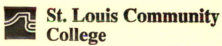

St. Louis Community College

Forest Park
Florissant Valley
Meramec

Instructional Resources
St. Louis, Missouri

THE DEATH PENALTY

Second Edition

THE DEATH PENALTY

ISSUES AND ANSWERS

By

DAVID LESTER, Ph.D.

Professor of Psychology
Richard Stockton State College
Pomona, New Jersey

CHARLES C THOMAS • PUBLISHER, LTD.
Springfield • Illinois • U.S.A.

Published and Distributed Throughout the World by

CHARLES C THOMAS • PUBLISHER, LTD.
2600 South First Street
Springfield, Illinois 62794-9265

© *1998 by* CHARLES C THOMAS • PUBLISHER, LTD.

ISBN 0-398-06822-4 (cloth)
ISBN 0-398-06823-2 (paper)

Library of Congress Catalog Card Number: 97-34267

First Edition, 1987
Second Edition, 1998

With THOMAS BOOKS *careful attention is given to all details of manufacturing
and design. It is the Publisher's desire to present books that are satisfactory as to their
physical qualities and artistic possibilities and appropriate for their particular use.*
THOMAS BOOKS *will be true to those laws of quality that assure a good name
and good will.*

Printed in the United States of America
MX-R-3

Library of Congress Cataloging in Publication Data

Lester, David, 1942-
    The death penalty : issues and answers / by David Lester. -- 2nd ed.
        p.   cm.
    Includes bibliographical references and indexes.
    ISBN 0-398-06822-4 (cloth). -- ISBN 0-398-06823-2 (paper)
    1. Capital punishment--United States. I. Title.
KF9227.C2L47   1997
345.73'0773--dc21   97-34267
                                                                                 CIP

For Alice Heim
who started me on my scholarly career

PREFACE

A great deal is written about the death penalty in popular magazines and newspapers in which the writers make definitive statements about research on the death penalty which have no basis in the scholarly literature. Even scholars occasionally make the same errors.

For example, it is common to read that the death penalty discriminates against African American offenders, and that the death penalty does deter murderers or, equally often, that the death penalty does not deter murderers.

The present book reviews the research conducted on the death penalty and examines what reliable conclusions can be drawn, if any, from this research. For example, research indicates that it is the race of the victim rather than the race of the offender that more often plays a role in sentencing a murderer to death.

This review also points out areas in which research is lacking. For example, there are no methodologically sound data on the economic cost of life imprisonment versus executing an offender.

The review attempts to be comprehensive; an effort was made to locate all research studies on the capital punishment. The first edition of this book reviewed research published up until 1984; this second edition has added research published up to 1995 and has included a few studies missed in the first edition.

CONTENTS

THE DEATH PENALTY

Chapter 1

INTRODUCTION

Arguments for Capital Punishment	Arguments Against Capital Punishment
It is a deterrent.	It is not a deterrent.
It prevents recidivism.	Murderers rarely murder again.
It is a moral duty.	It is morally wrong.
It is more economical than life imprisonment.	It is less economical than life imprisonment.
It is kinder than life imprisonment.	It is cruel and inhumane.
Those executed are the worst offenders and beyond rehabilitation.	Those executed are not beyond rehabilitation.
Those executed are less than human.	Those executed may have potential as humans, at least in some areas.

These arguments for and against capital punishment are well known. This particular set of arguments is based on lists provided by Turnbull (1978). They illustrate what is so fascinating about scholarly and intellectual debates on the death penalty. Both sides make parallel arguments!

Many socio-psychological issues are argued very differently. There is one set of arguments for one position and a different set of arguments for the alternative position. Resolution of the debate depends upon the relative importance attached to the different arguments. For example, if eighteen-year-olds are old enough to vote and be killed in war, how can they not be old enough to buy an alcoholic drink? Yet car accidents are reduced if the drinking age is raised. How do you weigh these two arguments?

For many of the arguments made for or against the death penalty there are no research data that are pertinent. Research cannot resolve moral dilemmas, but research should be able to throw light on some issues. Is the death penalty a deterrent? How harsh is prison, especially on death row? Are those executed different from other murderers? What is the attitude of the general public toward the death penalty?

This book will address these and other issues. The research will often fail to provide a clear and concise answer to some of the questions. But sometimes it will suggest a potential answer, one that may be more clearly answered in subsequent research.

The first edition of this book was published in 1987 and was a review of the scholarly literature on the death penalty up until 1984. A great deal of research has appeared since 1984, and this second edition incorporates the results of this recent research and modifies the conclusions drawn in the first edition where appropriate.

Social science research is not value free. The beliefs and the values of the researcher can affect the design of the research and the interpretation of the results. It can also affect the presentation and conclusions drawn by the author in a review of the literature. It is, therefore, important that reviewers make their biases clear to the reader. Consequently, I state here that, at present, I am in favor of the death penalty in the United States of America.

REFERENCE

Turnbull, C. Death by decree. *Natural History*, 1978, 87(5), 51-66.

Chapter 2

THE DEATH PENALTY
AROUND THE WORLD

In general, nations in South America, the Caribbean and Western Europe (plus Israel and Canada) have abolished the death penalty (United Nations, 1980b).

Wiechman et al. (1989, 1990) reviewed the status of death penalty around the world. From 1962 to 1983, about 85% of nations had the death penalty in some form. In the period from 1980 to 1985, 77% of 163 nations had a death penalty and 22 nations executed at least one person. However, by 1987, this percentage had dropped to 64%. (The number of nations in the world rose from 128 in 1960 to 172 in 1987.) For the 22 nations who executed prisoners in the period 1980-1985, the mean number executed was 4.2.[1]

Twenty nations were abolitionist in 1979 for all crimes:

Austria	Honduras
Brazil	Iceland
Colombia	Luxembourg
Costa Rica	Nicaragua
Denmark	Norway
Dominican Republic	Panama
Ecuador	Portugal
Fiji	Sweden
Finland	Uruguay
Federal Republic of Germany	Venezuela

---

1. Patrick (1965) has presented data on the status of the death penalty in nations of the world in the 1960s.

Twelve nations were retentionist for "non-ordinary" crimes:

Canada	New Zealand
Israel	Peru
Italy	Seychelles
Malta	Spain
Nepal	Switzerland
Netherlands	United Kingdom

Three federated nations were retentionist in some jurisdictions:
Australia
Mexico
USA

The remaining 121 nations of the world were retentionist.

Correlates of Having a Death Penalty

Wiechman et al. (1990) found that the death penalty was more likely to be in force in a nation in the early 1980s if the nation had a larger population under the age of 15 and a smaller population aged 65 or more, a lower gross national product per capita, fewer urban residents and a higher death rate–that is, were more underdeveloped. Population density was not associated with the presence of a death penalty.

Alcock and Eckhardt (1974) defined compassion as an attitude in which one places value on the use of reason or persuasion to guide human behavior as opposed to the use of threats, force or punishment. Alcock and Eckhardt attempted to measure this variable in nations of the world using five components: civil violence, land and income inequality, health and education, international cooperation and support for world order. Lester (1984) took a sample of 46 nations with ratings of compassion and compared the 26 abolitionist nations with the 23 retentionist nations. Lester found that the retentionist nations had lower compassion scores and, in particular, lower scores on the components of health and education, and support for world order. (The retentionist nations had less land income inequality, however.) Retentionist nations also had less freedom of the press, greater voting support for socialist parties and a lower gross national product per capita. The two groups of nations did not differ in the absence of civil violence, international cooperation, absence of international war, or voter support for communist or capitalist parties.

When Lester attempted to control for the gross national product per capita, the relation of the death penalty status to compassion disappeared. Lester concluded that the wealthier nations may be more concerned with the value of life. Increased wealth typically leads to increased leisure time and the financial resources for the pursuit of personal and hedonistic goals. As concern with the quality of life increases, concern with the value of life or others may also increase, reducing support for the death penalty.

Bowers (1974) conducted a study of 112 nations and found that the death penalty was more common where there was political centralization, political coerciveness and incomplete incorporation of non-associational groups. (Political instability and discrimination were not related to the presence of the death penalty.) However, executions were most common where there was political instability. These same variables also predicted the abolition of the death penalty (political coerciveness and incomplete incorporation negatively, and political instability positively). Day and Day (1984) found no association between the presence of capital punishment and fertility rates in 19 industrialized nations of the world.

There are 321 non-literate or primitive societies whose customs are coded in the Human Relations Area Files at Yale University, and Lester and Tauber (1986) searched a sample of 132 of these files. Only one society contained a clear mention both that there was no death penalty and gave no examples of the informal or formal application of capital punishment. (A further nine societies had no mention of the death penalty, present or absent, and one had no data on punishment in the files.) Thus, the death penalty, formal or informal, seems to have been widespread in primitive societies.

The Methods Used for Execution

Schumacher (1990) reported that the most common method for execution in the nations of the world was hanging. However, Hillman (1993) noted that in 1989, 86 nations used shooting for execution, 78 hanging, seven stoning, and six beheading. (The United States uses electrocution, intravenous injections and gassing primarily.) He speculated on whether the condemned person suffered in each of these methods and felt that they did, with the exception of lethal injections.

Which Crimes Carry a Death Penalty?

The crimes carrying a death penalty vary greatly from nation to nation, of course. In some nations, the list of crimes is short—for example, in Samoa, only murder and treason carried a death penalty in 1984. In other nations the list is longer—for example, in Poland in 1984 the death penalty was possible for homicide, assault, rape, robbery and offenses against the state, including crimes particularly harmful to the nation's economy. In a recent survey, Schumacher (1990) found that murder and treason were the most common crimes for which a death penalty was an option.

In primitive societies, Turnbull (1978) noted that the death penalty is generally given for crimes that threaten the whole society, not necessarily for what we would call treason, but rather for actions that are "blasphemous," that invoke the wrath of Gods against the entire society. The execution is generally cast as an act of atonement rather than of retribution (and, we might add, often the offender shares the societal belief system and willingly dies in this act of atonement).

The United Nations

Members of the United Nations have shown a sustained interest in the death penalty. In recent years, resolutions have been passed to limit the application of the death penalty.

In 1971, The General Assembly passed resolution 2857 (XXVI):

> In order to guarantee fully the right to life, provided for in Article 3 of the Universal Declaration of Human Rights, the main objective to be pursued is that of progressive restricting the number of offenses for which capital punishment may be imposed, with a view to the desirability of abolishing this punishment in all countries. (United Nations, 1980a, p. 6)

As a result of this and other resolutions, the United Nations has had periodic conferences and reports concerned with the status of the death penalty in its member nations (United Nations, 1980b).

The Effects of Abolition on Homicide Rates

Archer et al. (1963) examined the experience of 14 nations which had abolished the death penalty, comparing homicide rates in the periods prior to and after the abolition. They found that increases and decreases were equally likely. Overall homicide rates increased 7 percent from the five-year pre-abolition period to the five-year post-abolition period, but other crimes increased much more (rape 23 percent and theft 22 percent).

Discussion

Lingle (1993) noted that there is widespread condemnation in European and other industrialized nations of American enforcement of the death penalty, although many of these same nations have conscripted armies. Lingle saw little morally different between the death penalty and the coercion of young men and women into military service at "slave wages" in the course of which they may be killed–in war or even in "peacekeeping" missions.

Hartung (1952) suggested that several trends were apparent over the years in capital punishment: a move toward the abolition of capital punishment, a reduction in the number of capital offenses, the death sentence becoming discretionary rather than mandatory, the number of executions being reduced, a move from public to private executions and a move toward more swift and painless methods.

There are no reliable data on whether the death penalty generally deters murder in nations, though the study by Archer et al. (1963) is a promising first step in this direction.

REFERENCES

Alcock, N., & Eckhardt, W. An evaluation of compassion among nations. *Peace Research*, 1974, 6(1), 14-26.

Archer, D., Gartner, R., & Beittel, M. Homicide and the death penalty. *Journal of Criminal Law and Criminology*, 1983, 74, 991-1013.

Bowers, W. *Executions in America.* Lexington: D.C. Heath, 1974.

Day, L., & Day, A. Fertility and "life chances." *International Journal of Comparative Sociology*, 1984, 25, 197-225.

Hartung, F. Trends in the use of capital punishment. *Annals of the American Academy of Political and Social Science*, 1952, #284, 8-19.

Hillman, H. The possible pain experienced during execution by different methods. *Perception*, 1993, 22, 745-753.

Lester, D. An international study of the death penalty. *Peace Research*, 1984, 16(1), 35-37.

Lester, D., & Tauber, D. The death penalty in primitive societies. Unpublished, 1986.

Lingle, C. Human rights, military conscription, and capital punishment. *Current Politics and Economics of Europe*, 1993, 3(1), 43-48.

Patrick, C. The status of capital punishment. *Journal of Criminal Law, Criminology and Police Science*, 1965, 56, 397-411.

Schumacher, J. E. An international look at the death penalty. *International Journal of Comparative and Applied Criminal Justice*, 1990, 14, 307-315.

Turnbull, C. Death by decree. *Natural History*, 1978, 87(5), 51-66.

United Nations. *UN norms and guidelines in criminal justice.* New York: United Nations, 1980a.

United Nations. *Human rights questions: Capital punishment.* New York: United Nations, 1980b.

Wiechman, D., Kendall, J., & Bae, R. The death penalty. *Howard Journal*, 1989, 28, 124-137.

Wiechman, D., Kendall, J., & Bae, R. International use of the death penalty. *International Journal of Comparative and Applied Criminal Justice*, 1990, 14, 239-260.

Chapter 3

EXECUTIONS IN THE UNITED STATES

Modern government statistics on capital punishment begin in 1930, and executions temporarily ended in 1967. Who was executed during this period of 1930–1967? The U.S. Department of Justice (1981) has presented data on executions in the United States and publishes an annual report on capital punishment.[1]

The number of executions was highest in the 1930s and declined thereafter. California, Georgia, New York, North Carolina and Texas all executed more than 200 persons during this period, while Maine, Michigan, Minnesota, North Dakota, Rhode Island and Wisconsin executed no one. Of those executed, 99.2 percent were male and 53.5 percent were black. The crime was murder for 83.4 percent of the offenders.

Schneider and Smykla (1990) found that executions in the United States decreased during and after both world wars and after the Korean War. However, they did not carry out any statistical tests of significance on their data.

French (1987) examined the Espy file of executions in America from 1608 to 1985. Fifty-seven percent of those executed were black, ranging from 62% for those aged 12–20 to 23% for those 61 years of age and older. The percentage of blacks among the executed was higher in the South (79%) than in the non-South (31%). For the period 1930–1967, 89% of rapists executed were black as compared to 49% of the murderers executed.

Executions After 1977

Jolly and Sagarin (1984) presented data on the first eight people executed after the Supreme Court guidelines which permitted executions to take place in the United States again. From 1977 to 1983 eight

---

1. The Espy file (see below) lists all executions in the United States since 1608.

men were executed, seven white and one black. The average age was
35.1, and all eight were found guilty of murder and were almost certainly guilty. Seven of the men had long criminal histories.

Streib (1984) looked at the first eleven executions after 1977, of
whom nine were white and two black. Nine had prior convictions
(including two for murder), had committed their murder at the median age of 27 (range 22 to 44), and spent five years on death row (range
3 1/2 months to 10 years).

Culver (1985) looked at the first 32 executions after 1977. There
were 31 men and one woman executed; 72% were white and 28%
black; 26 had killed one victim and six more than one victim; 29 of
the executions took place in the South; and 14 of the offenders maintained their innocence.

Johnson (1985) presented data on the first 47 executions from 1977
to 1984: 60% were white, 36% black and 4% Hispanic. Johnson noted
that the proportion of murderers during this period was 35% white,
50% black and 15% Hispanic; the percentages of death row inmates
executed was 1.7% for whites and 1.1% for blacks; the percentages of
death row inmates with convictions or sentences overturned were 35%
for whites and 37% for blacks; and the percentages of murderers
arrested who were eventually sentenced to death were 1.6% for whites
and 1.2% for blacks. Johnson concluded that the criminal justice system seemed to be no longer biased against blacks as far as murder was
concerned. (More methodologically sound research on the issue of
racial disparity is reviewed in Chapter 7.)

From 1977 to 1990, 143 people were executed (Culver, 1992). Of
these, 142 were men, all were murderers or accomplices, and their
average age was 36.2 (with a range of 23 to 66). The lowest intelligence test score was 64, which is in the range commonly regarded as
retarded (below 70 in most educational systems). The men were 56%
white, 39% black and 5% Hispanic.

Regional Studies

Snyder (1992) examined 50 murderers executed in Texas from
1982 to 1992. Their mean age at execution was 36.4 years compared
to a mean age of 37.8 for their victims at the time of their murder. The
average time between the date of the crime and the date of the execution was 8.6 years.

Who Is Under Sentence of Death?

Marquart and Sorensen (1989) studied those inmates sentenced to death whose sentences were commuted after the 1972 *Furman* decision by the United States Supreme Court which halted executions in the United States until 1977. Of the 558 inmates on whom they had data, 85 percent had been sentenced to death for murder, 14 percent for rape, and one percent for armed robbery.

There were 714 prisoners under sentence of death at the end of 1980 (U.S. Department of Justice, 1981). In 1980, 187 persons were sentenced to death and 51 removed from death row. (In 1968, when executions were temporarily suspended, the number under sentence of death was 517.)

There were no federal prisoners under sentence of death in 1980. In the Northeast states, only Pennsylvania had prisoners under sentence of death; in the North Central states, only Indiana, Illinois, Missouri and Nebraska had prisoners under sentence of death. On the other hand, in the Southern states, only West Virginia did not have prisoners under sentence of death; in the West only Colorado, Alaska and Hawaii did not have prisoners under sentence of death.

Only eight (1.1%) of the 714 prisoners under sentence of death were female, and 282 (39.5%) were black. Of those receiving a death sentence in 1980, all 187 were for the crime of murder. Of those sentenced in 1980, 56 were aged 20 to 24 and 50 were aged 25 to 29. The vast majority of those receiving a sentence of death did not have any college education, and the most common marital status was "never married." Nine (6.0%) of those sentenced to death had prior convictions for criminal homicide out of 150 for whom this information was reported. (In 1981, 18 [9.4%] of those sentenced to death had prior convictions for criminal homicide out of the 191 offenders for whom this information was reported.)

Of the 714 prisoners on death row, the median length of stay was 25 months, with 38 having remained there for 72 months or more.

Carter and Smith (1969) noted that from 1935-1945 the average time spent on death row was 418 days, but by 1956–1962 it had risen to 843 days. The time from arrest to arrival on death row in 1956-1962 was 159 days. Blacks spent longer on death row than whites, who in turn spent longer than Mexican Americans.

Ekland-Olson (1988) examined death row inmates in Texas from 1974 to 1983 and noted that the number sentenced to die each year varied greatly during this period, from ten in 1974 to 42 in 1978 and 24 in 1983. Ekland-Olson compared death row inmates with non-death row inmates also convicted of murder and found that the death row inmates were more often men and more often whites, killing white victims, female victims and strangers. (The groups did not differ in the age of the offender or victim.) The death row inmates had more often raped their victims but had less often committed robbery or burglary along with the murder. The average time from arrest to conviction was 11.4 months with a range of two to 44 months. If the victim was white, the time was greater, but the characteristics of the offender played no role in this time.

In these ten years, 247 offenders were sentenced to death, 23 executed, three committed suicide and three died from other causes, and 149 remained on death row. Commutation of the death sentence was less likely if the murder involved rape or was the murder of a police officer, but victim characteristics and the race of the offender were not associated with commutation.

Smith and Felix (1986) studied 34 death row inmates in North Carolina. The modal inmate was black, 26 to 35 years of age, single, skilled and a Baptist. All had average intelligence. Twenty-three of them reported happy childhoods.

The Backgrounds of Those on Death Row

Lewis et al. (1986; Feldman et al., 1986) studied fifteen adult murderers on death row and found that all fifteen had suffered head injuries during their lives. Ten had cognitive dysfunctions, five major neurological impairment and a further seven minor neurological signs. Nine showed psychiatric symptoms in childhood, six were currently psychotic and three more episodically. Eight had been abused as children and four others had been brutally assaulted later.

State Variation in Statutes

Lester (1990) created an almost perfect Guttman scale for the breadth of the death penalty in the American states in 1965 (based on the range of crimes for which a death penalty was possible) using codings from Bedau (1967). The breadth of the death penalty statutes in the states was positively associated with the murder rate but not with the suicide rate.

Russell (1993) noted that the process for imposing a death sentence varies from state to state. For example, in Alabama, Florida and Indiana the jury recommends a sentence, but the judge can either accept it or override it.

States differ considerably in other characteristics such as the percentage of death sentences commuted by the state (Bedau, 1990-1991), state regulations concerning the provision and payment of lawyers for defendants (Wilson & Spangenberg, 1989), and the provision of mandatory death sentences for some offenses (Poulos, 1986).

Women and the Death Penalty

Rapaport (1990) noted that thirty women were executed from 1930 to 1967, of whom 70 percent were white. From 1978 to 1987, 39 women were sentenced to death, 21 had their sentences commuted, and one was executed.

Streib (1990a) studied 70 death sentences handed down to 67 women from 1973 to 1989, of whom one was executed. All of the death sentences were for murder, and these represented 1.8 percent of all death sentences. Sixty-seven percent of the women were white. At the end of 1989, 29 women were under sentence of death, all for murder, 66 percent of whom were white (as compared to 52 percent white for men). These women tended to be poor, uneducated and from the lower social classes.

Streib (1995a) examined the women sentenced to death from 1973 through to June 30, 1995. One hundred and seven women had been sentenced to death, some 2.0% of all death sentences, but the proportion has risen since 1989. Only forty-two of those sentenced to death currently remain on death row. One woman was executed and 64 sentences reversed or commuted. Twenty-three states have imposed these sentences, with Florida and North Carolina imposing a quarter. Sixty-four percent of the women were white and 29 percent were black.

Of those currently on death row, 60% are white, and the modal age is 21 to 30. Two-thirds of the victims were white and two-thirds men.

The forty-two women have been on death row for periods ranging from three months to over thirteen years.

Juveniles and the Death Penalty

Streib (1990b) noted that the 4,227 death sentences handed down in the United States from 1973 to 1990 included 101 juveniles–11 were 15 years old when they committed their crime, 23 were 16 years old and 67 were 17 years old. Only four of these juveniles had been executed.

At the end of 1990, thirty juveniles remained on death row. The modal age at the time of the crime was 17 years, 50 percent were white and 47 percent black, 69 percent of the victims were aged 18 to 49 years of age, 71 percent of the victims were white and 56 percent of the victims were female.

Streib (1995b) documented juveniles sentenced to death from 1973 through to June 30, 1995. Nine juveniles have been executed in this period, all aged 17 at the time of their crime. Of the 38 states and the federal government which permit executions, 14 jurisdictions have chosen 18 years as the minimum age for execution, four have set 17 as the age and 21 have chosen 16 as the age.

In this recent period, 140 juveniles have been sentenced to death (2.6% of all death sentences), only 42 of which are currently in force. There has been no trend in the numbers of juveniles sentenced to death over the period. Nine juvenile inmates have been executed and 89 sentences reversed or commuted. Texas and Florida have imposed the most juvenile death sentences (30 and 18, respectively). Fifty-one percent of the juveniles have been black and 40% white; 97% have been male and 3% female. Nine percent were aged 15 at the time of the crime, 21% aged 16, and 69% aged 17.

Of the 42 juveniles currently on death row, all were male and convicted for murder. Seventy-nine percent were 17 at the time of the crime and 21% were 16 years old; 48% were black and 33% were white. Their victims were primarily white (58%) but equally often male (51%) as female (49%).

Streib and Sametz (1989) noted that 282 juveniles had been executed in the history of the United States, including ten females. The last female juvenile executed was in 1912. These ten females had an average age of 15.4 years (versus 16.2 for male juveniles who were exe-

cuted); eight were black and one American Indian, and all their victims were white. Eight were executed for murder and two for theft.
Of the 398 adult females executed in the United States, 66 percent
were black and 31 percent white. More recently, from 1978 to 1988,
44 death sentences have been passed on 41 adult females and four
juvenile females, of whom 73 percent were white.

What Backgrounds Do These Juveniles Have?

Lewis et al. (1988) studied fourteen juveniles on death row. Nine
were judged to have a major neurological impairment, seven psychotic disorders and four severe mood disorders. (The remaining three
had periodic paranoid ideation.) Eight had experienced severe central
nervous trauma earlier in their lives requiring hospitalization or creat-
ing permanent indentations in their skull. Only two had intelligence
test scores above 90. Twelve had experienced brutal physical abuse
and five had been sodomized by relatives.

Robinson and Stephens (1992) reported on 91 juveniles sentenced
to death from 1973 to 1991. Forty-nine percent had a troubled family
history and social background, 32 percent were psychologically dis-
turbed, 26 percent were retarded, 53 percent were indigents, and 20
percent were substance abusers.

Retarded Individuals and the Death Penalty

Reed (1993) compared twelve retarded murderers executed in the
United States in recent years with twelve retarded murderers whose
death sentences were commuted. Those executed were younger at the
time of the crime, more often killed white victims, were sentenced
more often prior to 1985, were less often currently or previously married, had higher intelligence test scores and more education, and were
more often in the Southern states (with the exception of Georgia) than
those whose death sentences were commuted. In a multiple regression analysis, only age predicted execution. (The variables which did
not differentiate the two groups included the race of the murderer,
time on death row, whether mentally ill, whether abused as a child, the
presence of brain damage, the violence of the crime, whether there
were accomplices, the gender of the victim, whether the murder

involved sexual assault, the victim's age or whether the victim was physically handicapped.)

Executions in the Military

Lilly (1997) noted that the United States military has executed 160 people since the 1930s. Seventy were executed in Europe during the Second World War, mainly for rape and mainly black soldiers. Nineteen soldiers were executed in the United States during this war. No soldiers have been executed since 1961. All of the army death row inmates are minorities.

Discussion

This chapter has presented some data on the extent to which executions have taken place in the United States in recent times and the characteristics of those who get sentenced to death and those who are executed. Researchers have given special attentions to juveniles, women and the retarded who are sentenced to death.

Aside from simple descriptive statistics, the only noteworthy research is that which has explored the personal history and psychiatric/neurological background of those on death row. This research has been methodologically poor, with small samples and no comparison groups (for example, a group of those sentenced to prison terms for the same types of crime).

REFERENCES

Bedau, H. *The death penalty in America.* Chicago: Aldine, 1967.

Bedau, H. A. The decline of executive clemency in capital cases. *New York University Review of Law and Social Change*, 1990-1991, 18, 255-272.

Carter, R., & Smith, A. The death penalty in California. *Crime and Delinquency*, 1969, 15, 62-76.

Culver, J. H. The states and capital punishment. *Justice Quarterly*, 1985, 2, 567-578.

Culver, J. H. Capital punishment, 1977-1990. *Sociology and Social Research*, 1992, 76, 59-62.

Ekland-Olson, S. Structured discretion, racial bias, and the death penalty. *Social Science Quarterly*, 1988, 69, 853-873.

Feldman, M., Mallouh, K., & Lewis, D. O. Filicidal abuse in the histories of 15 condemned murderers. *Bulletin of the American Academy of Psychiatry and the Law*, 1986, 14, 345-352.

French, L. A. Boundary maintenance and capital punishment. *Behavioral Sciences and the Law*, 1987, 5, 423-432.

Johnson, L. W. The executioner's bias. *National Review*, 1985, 37(22), 44.

Jolly, R. W., & Sagarin, E. The first eight after *Furman. Crime and Delinquency*, 1984, 30, 610-623.

Lester, D. Capital punishment, gun control, and personal violence (suicide and homicide). *Psychological Reports*, 1990, 66, 122.

Lewis, D. O., Pincus, J. H., Bard, B., Richardson, E., Prichep, L. S., Feldman, M., & Yeager, C. Neuropsychiatric, psychoeducational, and family characteristics of 14 juveniles condemned to death in the United States. *American Journal of Psychiatry*, 1988, 145, 584-589.

Lewis, D. O., Pincus, J. H., Feldman, M., Jackson, L., & Bard, B. Psychiatric, neurological, and psychoeducational characteristics of 15 death row inmates in the United States. *American Journal of Psychiatry*, 1986, 143, 838-845.

Lilly, J. R. Military justice. *ACJS Today*, 1997, 15(4), 11.

Marquart, J. W., & Sorensen, J. R. A national study of the *Furman* commuted inmates. *Loyola of Los Angeles Law Review*, 1989, 23, 5-28.

Poulos, J. W. The Supreme Court, capital punishment and the substantive criminal law. *Arizona Law Review*, 1986, 28, 143-257.

Rapaport, E. Some questions about gender and the death penalty. *Golden Gate University Law Review*, 1990, 20, 501-565.

Reed, E. F. *The Penry penalty*. Lanham, MD: University Press of America, 1993.

Robinson, D. A., & Stephens, O. H. Patterns of mitigating factors in juvenile death penalty cases. *Criminal Law Bulletin*, 1992, 28, 246-275.

Russell, K. K. Trial by jury, death by judge. *Dissertation Abstracts International*, 1993, 53A, 3684.

Schneider, V., & Smykla, J. O. War and capital punishment. *Journal of Criminal Justice*, 1990, 18, 253-260.

Smith, C. E., & Felix, R. R. Beyond deterrence. *Federal Probation*, 1986, 50(3), 55-59.

Snyder, M. L. Capital punishment in Texas. *Psychological Reports*, 1992, 71, 754.

Streib, V. L. Executions under the post-*Furman* capital punishment statutes. *Rutgers Law Journal*, 1984, 15, 443-487.

Streib, V. L. The death penalty for female offenders. *University of Cincinnati Law Review*, 1990a, 58, 845-880.

Streib, V. L. Excluding juveniles from New York's impending death penalty. *Albany Law Review*, 1990b, 54, 625-679.

Streib, V. L. Capital punishment of female offenders. Cleveland, OH: Cleveland State University, 1995a, unpublished.

Streib, V. L. The juvenile death penalty today. Cleveland, OH: Cleveland State University, 1995b, unpublished.

Streib, V. L., & Sametz, L. Executing female juveniles. *Connecticut Law Review*, 1989, 22, 3-59.

U.S. Department of Justice. *Capital Punishment, 1980.* Washington, DC: U.S. Government Printing Office, 1981.

Wilson, R. J., & Spangenberg, R. L. State post-*Furman* representation of defendants sentenced to death. *Judicature*, 1989, 72, 331-337.

Chapter 4

HOW SEVERE A PENALTY
IS THE DEATH PENALTY?

In psychological terms, the death penalty may be seen as too severe a punishment or, in legal terms, as cruel and excessive punishment. How might this question be explored? Two approaches have been suggested.

Ratings of the Severity of Punishment

Hamilton and Rotkin (1976) had members of the general public rate various punishments for their severity. The death penalty was rated as the most severe (with a score of 55.43), but a life sentence without parole was rated close behind at 40.14. Seven years in prison rated 3.62 and fifteen years in prison 6.63.

Severity ratings by those in favor of capital punishment were lower than those opposed to capital punishment for nearly all but the weakest sentences. However, those opposed to capital punishment rated life imprisonment without parole as more severe than a death sentence, though the sample sizes were quite small in this part of the study.

Hamilton and Rotkin (1979) again had people rate the severity of punishments. Two years in prison received a 1.0, three years in prison 1.5, life with parole after 25 years 8.0, life with no parole 13.6, and a death sentence 16.2. Overall, the severity given to life with no parole was not significantly different from the severity given to a death sentence. (These ratings were not significantly associated with the race, sex, income or age of the respondent.) The respondents were then presented with a list of various crimes. One percent advocated a death sentence for mugging, 6 percent for forcible rape, and 41 percent for a planned killing.

Sebba (1978) had students rate the severity of different punishments. The death penalty received a rating of 6.1 on a logarithmic scale, life imprisonment 5.9, ten years in prison 4.6 and one year in prison 3.1. He found that whites gave the death penalty (and other punishments too) higher scores than blacks and that juniors and seniors gave it higher scores than freshmen and sophomores.

Sebba and Nathan (1984) also had people judge the severity of different penalties. One year of probation was assigned a value of 1.0, and if a punishment was considered three times as severe, the respondents had to give it a score of 30. Police officers rated the death penalty as 1,000, life imprisonment as 999, and ten years of prison as 85. Probation officers rated these three penalties as 1,000, 998, and 302, respectively. However, prisoners rated them as 1,000,000, 10,000 and 7,000, while students rated them 999,992, 10,000 and 302, indicating that both groups viewed the death penalty as much more severe than life imprisonment.

Is a Death Sentence Excessive?

The Supreme Court in 1972 in *Furman v. Georgia* held that death penalty statues must have procedural protections against excessive and discriminatory sentences. How might excessive be defined?

Baldus et al. (1979-1980) suggested an approach that reviews sentencing decisions in a state and compares a current case against these earlier decisions. They suggested several approaches and illustrated them with data from California jury decisions during 1958-1966.

Their first suggestion was to identify salient features of a case and then match this current case with earlier cases with identical salient features. This is somewhat arbitrary because people might differ in identifying from a list of salient features. (Furthermore, in their illustration, they weighted the features unequally in an apparent arbitrary fashion in looking for matches.)

A second approach used multiple regression to identify which of 150 variables were related to juries' decisions and how the variables might be weighted. They identified 13 variables and statistically assigned them weights. For example, for motives, sex as a motive added 3.5 points, revenge zero points and any other motive 1.4 points. If a defendant had a criminal record, 2.2 points were added versus zero for no record. In this way, they could arrive at an overall culpability score.

The third approach combined computation of an overall culpability score with matching the current defendant to earlier defendants on the 13 variables found to be significant in the regression analysis.

Discussion

When people rate the severity of the death penalty, it is surprising to find that a death sentence is not seen as exceedingly severe as compared to a life sentence without parole. The finding by Hamilton and Rotkin (1976) that those opposed to the death penalty rate life sentences without parole as more severe than a death sentence is most surprising and needs to be replicated by other investigators. In contrast, prisoners in the study by Sebba and Nathan do see a death sentence as more severe than a life sentence. Thus, it appears that judgments about the severity of different sentences may differ greatly for offenders and for the general public.

REFERENCES

Baldus, D., Pulaski, C., & Woodworth, G. Quantitative methods for judging the comparative excessiveness of death sentences. *Iowa Advocate,* 1979-1980, Fall/Winter, 1-7.

Hamilton, V., & Rotkin, L. Interpreting the Eighth Amendment. In H. Bedau & C. Pierce (Eds.), *Capital punishment in the United States.* New York: AMS, 1976.

Hamilton, V., & Rotkin, L. The capital punishment debate. *Journal of Applied Social Psychology,* 1979, 9, 350-376.

Sebba, L. Some explorations in the scaling of penalties. *Journal of Research in Crime and Delinquency,* 1978, 15, 247-265.

Sebba, L., & Nathan, G. Further explorations in the scaling of penalties. *British Journal of Criminology,* 1984, 24, 221-249.

Chapter 5

LIFE ON DEATH ROW

It is rather surprising that so little research has been published on the conditions on death row and on the effects of death row on the inmates. Turnbull (1978) has given a brief description of several death rows he has visited, another description has been given by Lewis (1979), and Vogelman (1989) has described life on a death row in South Africa. Radelet et al. (1984) have written about the families of death row inmates, but they presented no quantitative data.

Research Studies

Johnson (1979, 1980) interviewed thirty-five men on death row and interpreted their responses as indicating powerlessness, fear and emotional emptiness, leading to a cumulative experience of "living death." Powerful though his descriptions are, he used no quantitative measures, and he did not compare death row to imprisonment in other settings.

Bluestone and McGahee (1962) studied nineteen murderers on death row and reported that they were not highly anxious or depressed. They described three major defense mechanisms used by these inmates. Denial was used most often, including isolation of affect, minimizing the gravity of their position and delusions of a prospective pardon. They also used projection (for example, delusions of persecution) and obsessive rumination–especially about appeals and religion.

Gallemore and Panton (1972) studied eight inmates on death row and found that five had adjusted adequately and three poorly. Over time, the inmates tended to use the defense mechanism of projection more often, to identify more with one another and to an antisocial lifestyle, and to complain more about their health.

Smith and Felix (1986) studied 34 inmates on death row in North Carolina. Twenty-five reported having pleasant dreams and only seven had a depressed mood. The major defenses shown were denial of guilt, a refusal to discuss the crime, and projection and rationalization (such as "I was framed" and "I killed because of my military training"). They showed little anxiety, guilt or depression, but religious beliefs were common. There was no evidence of the defense mechanisms of sublimation, repression, displacement, idealization and symbolization.

Brown (1972) found no differences between the fear of death of death row inmates and of correctional officers. Lester and Alexander (1971) reported a guard from the death row at Sing Sing Prison as saying that, in joint executions, the men opted to be executed first, before the women.

Dahlstrom et al. (1986) gave inmates the MMPI while they were on death row in North Carolina and after their death sentences had been commuted to life imprisonment. The MMPI profiles indicated less disturbance after this change in sentence, particularly scores on the Schizophrenia scale. Eighteen of the profiles became healthier, while nine became less healthy.

Vogelman et al. (1994) reported a case of a South African inmate on death row who was pardoned and freed, and they claim that his psychological state after release resembled post-traumatic stress disorder.

Suicide and Murder on Death Row

Lester (1986) calculated that the suicide rate in prisons in general in 1978 to 1979 was 24.6 per 100,000 per year and the homicide rate was 29.4. For death row from 1977 to 1982 the suicide rate was 146.5 and the homicide rate was 73.3. These rates are remarkably high given the intense security provided for those on death rows.

Discussion

Little quantitative research has been conducted on those living on death row, a surprising omission since the quality of life on death row is an important issue for our assessment of whether execution is excessively cruel. Hopefully this omission will be remedied in the near future.

REFERENCES

Bluestone, H., & McGahee, C. Reactions to extreme stress. *American Journal of Psychiatry*, 1962, 119, 393-396.

Brown, D. The fear of death and the Western-Protestant ethnic personality identity. *Dissertation Abstracts*, 1972, 32B, 7302-7303.

Dahlstrom, W. G., Panton, J. H., Bam, K. P., & Dahlstrom, L. E. Utility of the Megargee-Bohn MMPI typological assignments. *Criminal Justice and Behavior*, 1986, 13, 5-17.

Gallemore, J., & Panton, J. Inmate response to lengthy death row confinement. *American Journal of Psychiatry*, 1972, 129, 167-172.

Johnson, R. Under sentence of death. *Law and Psychology Review*, 1979, 5, 141-192.

Johnson, R. Warehousing for death. *Crime and Delinquency*, 1980, 26, 545-562.

Lester, D. Suicide and homicide on death row. *American Journal of Psychiatry*, 1986, 143, 559-560.

Lester, D., & Alexander, M. More than one execution. *Journal of the American Medical Association*, 1971, 217, 215.

Lewis, P. Killing the killers. *Crime and Delinquency*, 1979, 25, 200-218.

Radelet, M., Vandiver, M., & Berardo, P. Families, prisons and men with death sentences. *Journal of Family Issues*, 1983, 4, 593-612.

Smith, C. E., & Felix, R. R. Beyond deterrence. *Federal Probation*, 1986, 50(3), 55-59.

Turnbull, C. Death by decree. *Natural History*, 1978, 87(5), 51-66.

Vogelman, L. The living dead. *South African Journal on Human Rights*, 1989, 5, 183-195.

Vogelman, L., Lewis, S., & Segal, L. Life after death row. *South African Journal of Psychology*, 1994, 24, 91-99.

Chapter 6

ATTITUDES TOWARD THE DEATH PENALTY

The attitudes held by people toward the death penalty is the topic on which there are the most studies published. In this chapter, the studies will each be briefly described (in alphabetical order) and then their conclusions summarized in the following section.

The Research Up Until 1984

Alston (1976) found that in the 1960s, Americans were more in favor of abolishing capital punishment than were the Japanese. In both nations, Alston reported that in males the younger and the more educated were more in favor of abolition, but he did not present any statistical tests of significance for these conclusions.

In a survey of American Bar Association members and students (Anon, 1982), support for the death penalty was found to be stronger in males, in the Southwest and prairie states, in older subjects, in those earning more, and in those who were regular members (rather than students). The size of their firm, the size of their city and their area of specialization were not related to attitudes toward capital punishment.

Balogh and Moeller (1960) found that policemen were more in favor of capital punishment than were other people.

Beswick (1970) gave various attitude scales to people in Australia. He found that opposition to capital punishment was related to opposition to mercy killing and war, but not to abortion. Those in favor of capital punishment were more ethnocentric. Gender, political affiliation and education were unrelated to attitudes toward capital punishment, but younger subjects and executives and professionals were more opposed to capital punishment.

Bibby (1981) surveyed Canadians and found that 78 percent favored capital punishment. Support for capital punishment increased with income and decreased with education. Gender, age, community size and church attendance were not related to attitudes.

Bronson (1970) gave prospective jurors a scale to measure their proneness to convict defendants and found that those in favor of capital punishment obtained higher scores on the scale of conviction proneness. Support for capital punishment was stronger in whites, males, Southern Baptists, Republicans, those with higher incomes and in skilled, white collar and professional workers. (Age was not significantly related to support for capital punishment, and the effect of education was non-linear.)

Colman and Gorman (1982) found that British policemen were more in favor of capital punishment than were civilians.

Combs and Comer (1982) found that whites supported capital punishment more than blacks, and that support increased during the 1970s for both races. Fear of walking in one's neighborhood was unrelated to support for capital punishment among whites but was associated with increased support among blacks. The amount of television watched was unrelated to support for capital punishment for both races, but exposure to newspapers was associated with increased support for capital punishment in both races. Conservative whites supported capital punishment more, and the same was true for blacks in 1974, but by 1980, political ideology was unrelated to support for capital punishment in blacks. Whites with higher incomes supported capital punishment more. The same was true for blacks in the early 1970s, but by the later 1970s the association was reversed for blacks.

Curtis and Lambert (1976) found that more educated Canadians were less socio-politically conservative as measured by a four-item scale which included an item on support for capital punishment.

Curtis and Perkins (1979) found in a sample of residents and college students that capital punishment was favored more by whites, those aged 55 and over, the single and separated, Protestants and Catholics, and males (though females were more in favor of capital punishment for rape).

DeFronzo (1979) found that support for capital punishment was positively related to a fear of crime but negatively related to experience of victimization (even after controls for race and political orientation were introduced).

Ellsworth and Ross (1983) asked respondents nine "factual" questions about the death penalty (though others might question the answers that they considered to be correct). The correct answers were chosen less often than the incorrect answers, but opponents of the death penalty were more often correct than proponents (which is the way that Ellsworth and Ross biased their definition of a correct answer). Proponents of the death penalty were less in favor of the constitutional guarantees of due process than opponents of the death penalty.

Erskine (1970) reported public opinion polls from the USA and other nations. One trend she identified was that support for capital punishment dropped in the USA from 1936 to 1966 and then rose in 1969.

Feather (1975) reported on a scale of conservatism which included an item on support for the death penalty. A factor analysis showed it to be loaded on a cluster of variables labeled as punitiveness.

Glenn (1974-1975) compared polls in 1953 and 1969. He found that whites favored the death penalty more than blacks, but that both groups favored the death penalty less in 1969. However, from 1953 to 1969, the difference between the views of whites and blacks grew.

Analyzing data from NORC polls, Granberg and Granberg (1981) found that support for capital punishment was only weakly related to attitudes toward abortion (though in the direction of a pro-life attitude). They did not report the sample size or statistical significance of their data.

Jepson (1959) in adult British students found that support for the death penalty was positively related to seeing homosexuality as a crime. People in different occupations differed in their support for the death penalty, with police officers most in support and social workers least in support.

Johnson and Newmeyer (1975) studied the voting patterns in San Francisco precincts in 1972 on two propositions, one on capital punishment and one on punishment for marihuana. The two voting patterns were very strongly related. Support for capital punishment was strongest in the lower middle class precincts. The votes for that proposition correlated positively with the median gross income, the proportion of owner-occupied homes and the proportion of elderly in the population and negatively with the proportion of single males and females, the proportion of college graduates and the proportion of professionally employed people.

Jurow (1971) found that people in favor of capital punishment were more conservative in political attitudes, more authoritarian, and more punitive in their sentencing decisions for cases presented to them.

Lester (Appendices 1 and 2) found that attitudes toward capital punishment were unrelated to gender. Those in favor of capital punishment favored more severe punishment for rape, but did not score higher on a general pro-rape scale.

In a survey of attitudes among the general public, Lotz and Regoli (1982) found that those in favor of capital punishment tended to agree with all rationales for it: retribution, deterrence and incapacitation. Those in favor of capital punishment also saw crime as a more serious problem, were more authoritarian, supported stronger discipline for youths, and were more opposed to rights, favors and privileges for prisoners.

McKelvie and Daoussis (1982) found that male students were more in favor of capital punishment than females and that extroverts were more in favor than introverts. McKelvie (1983) replicated this result, but found that attitudes toward capital punishment were not related to scores on measures of neuroticism or psychoticism.

In South Africa, Midgley (1974) interviewed whites and found that 57 percent supported capital punishment. Support was stronger in females, the older, the less educated, business owners and Protestants and Catholics.

Morsbach and Morsbach (1967) studied white students in South Africa and found that support for capital punishment was stronger in law students than in divinity students and stronger in the Afrikaans students than in the English-speaking students.

Moyser and Medhurst (1978) found that active church-goers in Britain were more in favor of abolishing capital punishment than those who were only nominally Anglican. The elite clergy, however, were even more in favor of abolition.

Musgrave and Reid (1971) asked 11- and 12-year-old children in Scotland what kinds of killing were wrong. One-sixth said that capital punishment was wrong. Those with higher intelligence test scores and those from the middle class (as compared to those from the working class) were more likely to mention capital punishment in this context.

Neapolitan (1983) found that students in favor of capital punishment said that they would be more willing to kill for money, less willing to turn the other cheek to aggression, had shown more prior aggressive behavior, showed less respect for the law and less fear of punishment, and showed less sympathy for victims of murder. They seemed generally aggressive people. Those favoring the death penalty for reasons of retribution were more extreme in these positions than those favoring the death penalty for reasons of deterrence.

Perkes and Schildt (1979) found that, among seventh, eighth and ninth graders, males were more in favor of capital punishment than females. The genders did not differ in whether they thought capital punishment was cruel and unusual punishment.

Rankin (1979) looked at NORC survey data and found that support for capital punishment was associated with voting for Nixon or Wallace in the 1968 and 1972 elections, support for spending money to fight crime, a law and order position, and owning a gun, but not with fear of victimization.

Ray (1982) reported on the percent supporting capital punishment in various nations of the world. Support ranged from 55 percent in Australia to 76 percent in Scotland. In South Africa, manual workers favored the death penalty more, as did those with authoritarian personalities. Ray found no differences by age, gender, education or Afrikaans/English.

Ruggiero and Weston (1977) found that males favored the death penalty more than females in the United States in a national poll in 1974. However, the difference was significant only for whites, those aged 30 to 40, those presently married and those attending church regularly. The gender difference disappeared when Ruggiero and Weston controlled for occupation.

Sawyer (1982) found that support for capital punishment was related to support for euthanasia and for suicide (but not for abortion). He concluded, therefore, that there was fairly good evidence for a consistent attitude toward taking life.

Smith (1978) looked at national polls from 1972 to 1977 and noted that support for capital punishment increased during that period, regardless of the group conducting the poll.

Snortum and Ashear (1972) had people give sentences ranging from a few years, through life, up to the death penalty for various cases of murder. The degree of punitiveness was only weakly related to age, education and gender (with older people, males and the less educated being more punitive). Punitiveness was not related to residential status. However, punitiveness was strongly related to attitudes toward police violence and to scores on a scale of anomic authoritarianism.

Starr (1983) found that college females were more opposed to capital punishment than males (and more opposed to other forms of violence as well, such as the use of nuclear weapons). Protestants were less opposed to capital punishment than Catholics or Jews. Those with the more educated fathers were more opposed to capital punishment, but family income was not linearly related to attitudes. Family socialization variables had no association with attitudes, except for the use of physical punishment after the age of five. Males punished physically were more in favor of capital punishment (whereas for females there was no association). A measure of traditional gender role orientation was not related to attitudes.

Stricker and Jurow (1974) found that college students who were opposed to capital punishment were less likely to assign the death penalty to cases of murder and were more liberal (versus conservative) in their general attitudes.

Swan (1983) reviewed polls and concluded that males supported capital punishment more than females among the general population and among American Bar Association lawyers and student members.

Thayer (1970) gave students questionnaires asking them whether, if they were jurors, they could give the death sentence. Those who could give it had a more punitive attitude toward criminals and felt more positive about the criminal justice system than those who could not give a death sentence. However, they did not differ in dogmatism or authoritarianism.

Thayer and Foster (1975) in a study of people in the community found that support for capital punishment was related to people's perception of the crime rate, their fear of victimization, their perception of the effectiveness of punishment, and their acceptance of punishment for criminal behavior.

Thomas and Howard (1977) gave an attitude inventory to a random sample of adults in a metropolitan area. They found that support for capital punishment was related to a positive assessment of the effectiveness of punishment, less support for fundamental civil liberties, and strong feelings in support of retribution. Support for capital punishment was only weakly associated with dogmatism, and this association became negative once other attitudes were controlled for.

Tyler and Weber (1982) found that support for the death penalty in community residents was not related to their history or fear of victimization, to socio-demographic variables (such as age, gender, race, education, income or religion), or to their liberalism, but only to their scores on a measure of authoritarianism.

Vidmar (1974) surveyed Canadians in 1972 and found that 78 percent favored the death penalty in some circumstances. The degree of support for the death penalty was higher in those who were more supportive of a retribution philosophy, more authoritarian, more dogmatic, more prejudiced, less educated, and older. The degree of support was not related to gender, marital status, occupation, regional, family income or fear of crime.

Watkins and Sampson (1975) found among Australian high school students that the males and the older students were more in favor of capital punishment than the females and the younger students.

For Which Crimes Should There Be a Death Penalty?

De Boer (1979) reported that the majority in the United States, the United Kingdom and West Germany were in favor of the death penalty for terrorists.

Ellsworth and Ross (1983) surveyed Californians and found that 59 percent favored capital punishment. When presented with a list of crimes, the death penalty was seen as most appropriate for mass murder and least for robbery with no deaths. As the crimes became less severe, people switched from supporting a mandatory death penalty to a discretionary one and then to no death penalty.

Lester (Appendix 1) found that police officers and college students agreed on the six crimes most deserving the death penalty: assassination of the president, a serial murderer, a person who tortures a victim prior to the murder, a person who kills several people at the same time, a person who murders someone else's child, and a person who kills a police officer.

Changing People's Attitudes Toward Capital Punishment

Lord et al. (1979) showed students in favor of or opposed to capital punishment results of research that claimed either to support the deterrent effect of capital punishment or to show no evidence of a deterrent effect. If they showed one piece of research to the students, their attitudes shifted toward the results of the research study. If they showed the students critiques of the research and rebuttals, the attitude shift disappeared. If they showed two pieces of research, the results of which were in conflict, then the students also shifted back to their original positions and became more extreme in them.

Roberts (1984) found that people who read an article on capital punishment remembered those parts of it more easily that were in accordance with their own views, and also distorted the conclusion of the article in their memory in line with their own views.

Sarat and Vidmar (1976) found that giving people information about the death penalty that focussed on research into its deterrent effect changed their attitudes, whereas information based upon humanitarian issues did not change their attitudes. Those people who were strongly in favor of retribution did not change their attitudes much at all, whereas those who were not strongly in favor of retribution became even less favorable toward capital punishment after reading the deterrence information.

Stages of Moral Development

Kohlberg and Elfenbein (1975) found that children's reasoning about capital punishment matched the stage of moral reasoning that the child was in. The correlation between the moral stage of development and the degree of opposition to capital punishment was large and positive (though it should be noted that the method of statistical analysis used was incorrect).

A Review of the Results

This set of studies revealed several consistent findings. Support for capital punishment was stronger in older people (seven studies versus three finding no association), the less educated (seven studies versus three finding no effect and one finding a non-linear relationship), in those earning more (six studies versus one showing no effect), whites (four studies versus one showing no differences), authoritarian attitudes (six studies with one finding no association), and conservatives (three studies plus one showing the results for whites only and one study finding no differences).

Gender differences were inconsistent. Ten studies found males more in favor of capital punishment, two studies found females more in favor of capital punishment (and a third study found this for rape), while six studies found no differences.

Two studies found decreasing support for capital punishment up to the late 1960s, and then three studies reported an increase in support during the 1970s.

By occupation, three studies reported that police officers were more in favor of capital punishment. Single studies reported less support in social workers, the elite clergy and divinity students, but more support in business owners, law students, manual workers, white collar workers and professionals. One study found no differences by occupation.

Support for capital punishment was stronger in Japan than in the United States and stronger in Great Britain than in Australia. In the United States, support for capital punishment was stronger in the Southwest and prairie states.

In single studies, support for capital punishment was associated with less educated fathers, more exposure to newspapers, being single and separated (while another study found no differences by marital status), owning a gun, experience of physical punishment, Afrikaans (versus English in South Africa, while another study found no differences), extroversion, and prejudice.

In addition, support for capital punishment was stronger in those favoring law and order, euthanasia, suicide, mercy killing, punitiveness (eight studies), and judging homosexuality to be a crime.

Support for capital punishment was related to ethnocentrism, positive views of the criminal justice system, opposition to rights for prisoners and guarantees of due process (three studies), pro-violence attitudes, and more aggressive and antisocial attitudes.

Support for capital punishment was not related to advocating a traditional gender role orientation, neuroticism, psychoticism, residential status, amount of television watched, the size of the community (two studies), and in lawyers the size of the firm and their specialty.

One study found dogmatism positively related to support for capital punishment while another found a negative relationship and a third no association. Support for capital punishment was inconsistently related to attitudes toward abortion (two studies found no difference while one found support for capital punishment to be related to support for abortion). Support for capital punishment was also inconsistently related to fear of crime and victimization (one study found no differences, four found a positive association and two found a negative association) and political affiliation (one study found no association while another found Republicans to be more in favor of the death penalty).

Religion was also inconsistently related to support for capital punishment. One study found active churchgoers more opposed to capital punishment, while two studies found no differences. Two studies found Protestants and Catholics to be more in favor of capital punishment, another found only Protestants to be more in favor, another found Southern Baptists to be more in favor, while two studies found no differences by affiliation.

The Research from 1985 to 1995

Aguirre and Baker (1984) found in a national sample of white Americans that support for the death penalty was stronger among older Americans, men and racists but was not associated with fear of victimization from crime.

Barkan and Cohn (1994) found that support for the death penalty in a general population survey of whites in 1990 was associated with political conservatism and antipathy to blacks, and was higher in men, the South and those with more education. Support for the death penalty was not associated with fear of crime, belonging to a fundamentalist church, church attendance or age.

Bohm (1992) found that college students who favored capital punishment believed more strongly in retribution (vindictive revenge rather than revenge utilitarianism). Bohm also found that whites were more in favor of capital punishment, but men and women did not differ in their attitudes.

Bohm et al. (1990) analyzed data from a survey in New York State and found that support for the death penalty was stronger in males, Hispanics, people from Long Island, those aged 18-24 and 60-64, Protestants, those with a high school diploma, those opposed to gun control, conservatives, and those concerned with crime and drugs. In Texas, McShane et al. (1987) found support for capital punishment to be stronger in males, whites and Hispanics and those with higher incomes.

Clagett and Austin (1986) studied passengers at three airports and found that 79 percent were in favor of capital punishment. Support for the death penalty was stronger in Texas and Louisiana than in New York, those with no college education, church members, Republicans, conservatives and whites. Occupation, urban/rural residence, and religious affiliation were not associated with support for the death penalty.

Claggett and Shafer (1991) examined data from national polls conducted for the *Times Mirror*. They found that approval of capital punishment and abortion were positively, but weakly, related. They did not analyze their data with appropriate statistical tests, and so it is hard to be sure what their exact findings are. However, it appears that this positive association was found for most groups in the population except for white, low church Protestants and for Republican activists.

Cullen et al. (19985) found that attitudes toward capital punishment in residents of a small town were associated with their attitudes toward punishment and rehabilitation, but not to victimization experiences. Their attitudes toward capital punishment were predicted by their gender and having a classical (rather than a positivist) view of the causation of crime. Age, education, and income were not related to attitudes toward capital punishment. Cullen also added a sample of criminal justice personnel to residents sample, and this changed the results somewhat, but also made them less meaningful. (It would have been better to analyze the data from the two samples separately.)

Curtis (1991) found that, among college students, Republican, religious fundamentalists and those with less faith in humans were more in favor of the death penalty.

De Vries and Walker (1986) found that the higher the stage of moral reasoning in college students, the more opposed to capital punishment they were–the students used their higher levels of moral reasoning to oppose capital punishment. De Vries and Walker (1987) found that the level of cognitive complexity was associated with the students' attitudes toward capital punishment, but in a non-linear manner. Those with extreme positions (either pro or con) were less cognitively complex than those with neutral positions on the issue.

Fagan (1986) found police officers in Washington State favored capital punishment more than did the general public. Police officer support for capital punishment was associated with their conservatism, support for police and prisons and lack of support for the courts, punitive attitudes regarding criminal sanctions, being male, coming from smaller cities, having less education, feeling that religion is important and being concerned about crime. (Marital status and income were not associated with attitudes toward capital punishment.)

Finlay (1985) looked at the results of the NORC General Social Survey in 1977 and 1978 and found that approval of capital punishment was positively associated with approval of euthanasia. Jews and fundamental Protestants were more in favor of the death penalty than those with other religions.

Fox et al. (1990-1991) looked at NORC polls and found that support was stronger in males, whites, the married, those with children, older respondents, Republicans and conservatives, those from the higher social classes, the more educated, those with higher incomes and in the West. (Religious affiliation was not associated with attitudes.)

Grasmick et al. (1993) found that Evangelical/Fundamentalist Christians were most in favor of the death penalty, followed by Roman Catholics, liberal Protestants, and finally those with no religious affiliation. Men, whites, those with a higher income, the less educated and Republicans were more in favor of the death penalty.

Hamm (1989) surveyed members of the Indiana state legislature and found that they supported capital punishment for adults more than for juveniles. Support for the death penalty was associated with being Republican, living in rural areas and fewer visits to prisons. However, the support of the legislators for capital punishment was probably less than that of residents in Indiana, according to Hamm. McGarrell and Sandys (1996) also studied Indiana legislators and found that the legislators believed that their constituents supported the death penalty over a life sentence without parole more than their constituents actually did. Indiana residents thought that their legislators would prefer a life sentence without parole more than their legislators actually did. So there does appear to be a conflict here between the two groups. Sandys and McGarrell (1994) found that support for the death penalty among Indiana legislators was less if they were offered a life sentence without parole as an alternative. The major predictors of the legislators' attitudes were their political orientation and their concern for reelection (and not gender, age, or whether employed in the criminal justice field).

Harris (1986) analyzed the results of a general poll in 1984 in which 27 percent of the respondents supported the death penalty for all cases of murder, 57 percent for some, 12 percent for none and 4 percent were undecided. Support for the death penalty varied with the crime, ranging from 84 percent for a brutal murder to 56 percent for murder of a prison guard. Support for the death penalty was higher in men, whites, high school graduates, Jews, Republicans and the wealthier. The most common reason for support was to protect society (42%), to deter others (31%) and to punish the murderer (17%). However, only 28 percent felt that the death penalty was fairly carried out, and 65 percent felt that minorities were more likely to be sentenced to death.

Harvey (1986) found that male undergraduate students were more in favor of the death penalty than women. Furthermore, conservatives and those attending church more frequently were also more in favor of the death penalty. Other correlates of attitudes included a belief in universal and absolute truths created by extrapersonal forces, strong religiosity, and holding conventional values.

Holden (1993) found that although members of a right-to-die organization (the Hemlock Society) and a pro-life organization (the California Pro-Life Council) differed in such beliefs as the existence of life after death, the same proportion supported capital punishment (about 72%).

Kelley and Braithwaite (1990) explored the attitudes of a national sample of Australians and found that support for the death penalty was greater among men, the married, the less educated, those anti-union, those who felt negatively toward minorities (such as aborigines and foreign-speaking immigrants), rating crime fighting as a national priority, feeling pessimistic about human nature, and if their state had abolished the death penalty. Fear of crime, age, urban/rural residence, political affiliation, economic conservatism and Christian belief were not associated with support for capital punishment.

Keil and Vito (1991) surveyed residents in Kentucky in 1989 and found that support for the death penalty was stronger among whites, men, high-income households and those who had a greater fear of neighborhood crime.

Larsen et al. (1990, 1991) found that attitudes toward capital punishment in college students were associated with having negative attitudes toward AIDS patients. This was found in American, Danish and

Norwegian students, even though the Scandinavian students were less supportive of capital punishment than were the American students.

Lester et al. (1990) examined students' judgments about the morality of several life/death issues. They found two clusters of judgments; suicide, refusal of medical treatment, abortion and euthanasia (actions involving the self) were viewed similarly in one cluster while war, capital punishment and cannibalism (actions involving others) were viewed similarly in the other cluster. Judgments of greater morality on this second cluster were associated with gender (males scored these behaviors as more moral) and negatively with measures of irrational thinking and neurotic tendencies. Judgments about the morality of the death penalty by itself were associated with lower scores on the measure of neurotic tendencies.

In a survey in Los Angeles, Mitchell and Sidanius (1993) found that support for capital punishment was associated with both conservatism and the desire for one's in-group to be socially dominant, and these associations were stronger in the residents of higher social status.

Moran and Comfort (1986) studied jurors who had served on juries for felony trials. Those who favored capital punishment were more authoritarian, younger, more often white and wealthier, Republican, and male. (Education was not associated with support for capital punishment.) Those in favor of capital punishment also saw themselves as more influential in the jury deliberations. (The juries on which they served were not necessarily murder trials.) Other correlates of attitudes appeared in only one of the two samples studied or in only those of one gender (correlates such as guilt-proneness, rigidity, marital status, owning a home, and having had unpleasant experience with the police).

Ross and Kaplan (1993-1994) found that attitudes toward capital punishment in undergraduates were not associated with liberal-conservative attitudes or having an intrinsic-extrinsic religious orientation. When asked about who "owns" our lives (God, the individual or the state), only the belief that the state owns our lives was associated with favoring the death penalty (negatively). Those in favor of the death penalty also were positive about suicide and assisted suicide, but did not differ in attitudes about abortion, though all of these attitudes were positively associated with one another.

Sebba and Nathan (1984) found that police officers were most in favor of the death penalty (50% in favor), followed by students (37%), probation officers (21%) and prisoners (0%).

In a survey of community residents, Seltzer and McCormick (1987) found that experience of victimization was not a predictor of attitudes toward the death penalty, but general fear of crime was associated with attitudes toward the death penalty, though in a non-linear manner (those with a moderate fear of crime supported the death penalty more).

Skovron et al. (1989) surveyed community residents by telephone about the death penalty for juveniles. In Columbus (OH) only 35% approved and in Cincinnati only 31%. Respondents were more in favor of the death penalty for adult offenders than for juveniles. In Cincinnati, only opinions about the effects of rehabilitation on offenders was associated with attitudes toward the death penalty; in Columbus gender and religiosity as well as opinions about the effects of rehabilitation were associated with attitudes toward the death penalty. (Religiosity was positively associated with favoring the death penalty, while the effect of gender was not specified in the report.)

Smith and Wright (1992) looked at the General Social Survey in the 1980s and found that support for the death penalty was stronger among men, whites, Republicans and the college educated and among those living in the West. Support was not consistently associated with age or religion (Protestant versus Catholic). Looking at whites alone, Smith and Wright found that the same variables predicted support for the death penalty, except now Protestants showed more support than did Catholics.

Stevens (1992) surveyed inmates in maximum and minimum security prisons about their attitudes toward the death penalty. Sixty-three percent of those in the maximum security prisons favored the death penalty in some form, as did 53 percent of those in the minimum security prisons. There were no differences in the opinions of violent and non-violent offenders.

Tygart (1994) found that California residents were more likely to favor the death penalty if they were male, conservatives, and believed in free will (versus societal problems) as the cause of murder. Age was not related to attitudes.

Warr and Stafford (1984) surveyed residents of Seattle and found that those who saw the goal of punishment as retribution or incapacitation were most in favor of the death penalty, while those who saw rehabilitation as more important were in favor.

Williams et al. (1988) found that support for capital punishment was higher among whites and men in a community sample in Texas.

Young (1991) interviewed a community sample in Detroit. Support for capital punishment was associated with race, income, education, with whites, the wealthier and the more educated more in support of the death penalty. For whites, a belief that poverty causes crime, that crime pays, education and income predicted support for the death penalty, while for blacks attitudes toward police power predicted support for the death penalty. Thus, clear ethnic differences emerged.

Young (1992) examined data from the General Social Survey and found that support for the death penalty was stronger among men and whites and was associated positively with conservatism and negatively with the religious orientations of devotionalism and evangelism. Support was not associated with age, education, region, or the religious orientations of fundamentalism, reborn and literalism. Looking at whites alone, the correlations with religious orientation changed—for whites, support for the death penalty was positively associated with fundamentalism and negatively with devotionalism.

In college students, Young and French (1992) found that students who agreed more with a list of "myths" about aggression (which were not defined by the authors) were more in support of the death penalty.

Changes Over Time

Fox et al. (1990-1991) looked at NORC polls and found an increase in support for capital punishment from 1972 to 1985, peaking in 1983.

Looking at national polls about attitudes toward capital punishment, Danigelis and Cutler (1991) found that, not only did support for it grow from 1958 to 1985, support increased within cohorts (even after adjustment for gender and education).

Smith and Wright (1992) examined public opinion polls and noted that support for the death penalty increased from 1972 on in America.

Ellsworth and Gross (1994) noted that national polls indicated a growing support for the death penalty in Americans since 1970. Warr (1995) also documented from national polls increasing public support for the death penalty from 1960 to 1994. Anon (1985) found that national support for the death penalty grew from 1965 to 1983; with the majority of respondents viewing it as a deterrent, preferring lethal injection over other methods, believing that blacks were not more likely to be sentenced to death but that the poor were more likely to receive a death sentence.

Zeisel and Gallup (1989) looked at Gallup polls on capital punishment from 1936 to 1986. Support declined from 61 percent in 1936 to 42 percent in 1966, rising thereafter to 70 percent in 1986. Support for the death penalty in 1986 was stronger in men, Republicans, the wealthier, whites, those with high school education and those in the West.

Correlates of Regional Attitudes

Handberg and Unkovic (1985) found that states in 1936 which had more public support for the death penalty had higher murder rates and a higher execution rate.

Methodological Issues

Williams et al. (1988) examined the effect of the phrasing of the question on people's responses. Using a community sample in Texas, they found that the use of the phrase "death penalty" rather than "capital punishment" did not affect people's responses. However, support for capital punishment was stronger for the abstract situation than for specific cases presented to the respondents. Support for capital punishment was dependent also upon the type of crime committed by the offender.

Similarly, in a sample of college students, Smith (1987) found that 79 percent supported capital punishment in general. However, a majority of the supporters were in favor of a restricted application. When presented with specific cases, the percentage in favor of the death penalty varied from 31 percent to 98 percent for the individual cases.

Jones (1994) documented that support for the death penalty depended greatly on the phasing of the question. Permitting "don't know" or "no opinion" as a response affected the degree of support;

females and African Americans were more likely to choose such an option than males and whites.

Bowers (1993) reviewed data from several national surveys and found that the majority favored capital punishment. However, if the respondents were asked to choose between a death sentence and a life sentence without parole, the majority preferred a life sentence without parole. This particular result was replicated in an Indiana sample by McGarrell and Sandys (1996). Bowers also found that the majority of the general public and jurors qualified for capital trials believed that the death penalty is administered in too arbitrary a fashion. He also found that the general public and jurors underestimated the length of prison time served by murderers, but for this comparison Bowers used the time for which the murderers are sentenced rather than data on the actual time served by convicted murderers. McGarrell and Sandys (1996) also replicated this result in Indiana.

Sandys and McGarrell (1995) surveyed Indiana residents and found that 76 percent favored capital punishment. However, if presented with alternatives such as life without parole, only 45 percent supported capital punishment. The majority opposed capital punishment for the mentally retarded and for juveniles. Support for capital punishment was higher in whites, males, conservatives, those who rented homes, those who felt safe in their neighborhoods and those opposed to rehabilitation for criminals.

Polarization

Miller et al. (1993) gave college students who were opposed to or in favor of capital punishment two essays to read, one supporting and one opposing capital punishment. They found that the essay judged to be more persuasive was the one in line with the students' own opinion. In addition, reading the two articles increased the strength of belief of the students, that is, the students' attitudes became more polarized. Interestingly, this polarization did not occur when the experiment was repeated using attitudes toward affirmative action. Thus, attitudes toward capital punishment seem to follow different psychological rules than other attitudes.

Stamm and Dube (1994) found that those most opposed and most in favor of the death penalty held those views with more intensity, involvement and closed-mindedness than those with more intermediate views, a phenomenon found in other attitudes too (such as attitudes regarding health insurance and wetland protection). Those in favor of capital penalty placed more trust in the television news than those opposed.

The Stability of Attitudes

Kristiansen and Zanna (1991) found that attitudes of college students, tested two months apart, were more stable than attitudes toward affirmative action. They also found that the students' attitudes toward capital punishment were related to the importance they placed on values they considered relevant to their own lives, but only the attitudes toward capital punishment of those who scored high on a test of self-monitoring were related to the importance they placed on values that they considered irrelevant to their own lives.

The Impact of Indoctrination

Bohm et al. (1991) gave undergraduate students a myths about the death penalty scale. (An inspection of the items shows that the authors were biased–there are items about whether the death penalty deters and about its cost, issues which we can see from this book are the subjects of great debate.) Scores on this scale did not differ with gender, race or social class. On retesting, ordinary students showed no change in scores, whereas students in a course on the death penalty became more opposed to the death penalty after the class and obtained a lower "myths" score. The change in attitudes toward the death penalty among the students enrolled in the course on the death penalty was greater for those most in favor of the death penalty at the beginning of the class. Those who were least in favor of retribution as a principle at the beginning of the class also changed their attitudes more as a result of the class.

In a (presumably) second study, Bohm (1990) found that students in a class on the death penalty did not change their opinions any more or less than comparison students in a regular class. In the death penalty class, however, females, blacks and non-criminal justice majors were more opposed to the death penalty after the class than before.

Bohm (1989) showed that the course he taught on capital punishment led to the students becoming more opposed to the death penalty, while a later study (Bohm et al., 1990) showed that a course on the death penalty had little impact on students' opinions. Since Bohm gives no details as to the content and orientation of the courses, these studies are of little value.

Bohm and Vogel (1993) compared students who took a course on the death penalty (which again was apparently biased against the death penalty) with students who did not take the course. The initial change in opinions about the death penalty in those taking the course (a change toward more opposition) was not apparent two to three years later when the students were retested. Bohm et al. (1994) found that in both groups of students, the same variables predicted death penalty opinions, such as race (with whites favoring the death penalty more) and correctional philosophy (with those emphasizing revenge, incapacitation and deterrence favoring the death penalty more).

Conclusions

The conclusions of the last ten years of research into attitudes toward capital punishment are largely in agreement with the results of the earlier research. Support for capital punishment has clearly increased through the 1980s. Twenty-one studies found that men support capital punishment more than women do, while only two studies found no gender differences. Fifteen studies found that whites support capital punishment more than blacks do, while two studies also found that Hispanics are more in favor of capital punishment.

Other strong correlates of support for capital punishment included racism (three studies), conservative attitudes (ten studies, with only one finding no association), higher income (eight studies, with only two finding no association), and Republican political affiliation (eight studies).

Conflicting results were found for age (three studies found a positive association, one a negative association, one a non-linear association and five no association), education (six studies found a negative association, three a positive association and three no association), urban/rural location, and religion.

Other possible associations, based however on only one or two studies, included Southern/Western states, support for retribution and opposition to rehabilitation for offenders, opposition to gun control, concern with crime as a social problem, a belief in free will, less faith in people, and a negative attitude toward people with AIDS.

No support was found for an association with marital status, occupation (except that police officers support capital punishment more), victimization experiences, or fear of crime.

Discussion

There has clearly been a great deal of research into attitudes toward capital punishment and their correlates. Several consistent findings have been reported, but the importance of these findings is questionable. For example, the fact that men support capital punishment more than women is of only minor interest.

The most interesting results come from surveys which have varied the format for the questions, indicating that many respondents, who appear to favor the death penalty when presented with a simple yes/no answer format, prefer mandatory life sentences when presented with that alternative.

However, Bowers' (1993) report that respondents underestimate the length of time served by murderers who are not executed was methodologically unsound. He looked at the length of the sentence handed down, not the actual sentence served. First, most death sentences do not result in executions; why then should the public believe that a life sentence would mean that the murderer would never be released? Second, in the mid-1980s, only 17 percent of murderers sentenced to prison were sentenced to life; the remainder were sentenced to an average of 16 years (Lester, 1991). Clearly, we need more recent data on the sentencing patterns for murder. Finally, there are few data available on the actual time served by murderers, both in absolute terms and also in relation to the sentence handed down. More data on these issues would be of great interest.

REFERENCES

Aguirre, A., & Baker, D. V. Racial prejudice and the death penalty. *Social Justice*, 1993, 20, 150-155.

Alston, J. Japanese and American attitudes toward the abolition of capital punishment. *Criminology*, 1976, 14, 271-276.

Anon.   ERA, handgun control and the death penalty.   *American Bar Association Journal,* 1982, 68, 266-267.

Anon.   The death penalty considered.   *Public Opinion,* 1985, 8(3), 38-39.

Balogh, J., & Moeller, M.   A scaling technique for measuring social attitudes toward capital punishment.   *Sociology and Social Research,* 1960, 45, 24-26.

Barkan, S. E., & Cohn, S. F.   Racial prejudice and support for the death penalty by whites.   *Journal of Research in Crime and Delinquency,* 1994, 31, 202-209.

Beswick, D.   Attitudes toward taking life.   *Australian and New Zealand Journal of Sociology,* 1970, 6, 120-130.

Bibby, R.   Crime and punishment.   *Social Indicators Research,* 1981, 9(1), 1-13.

Bohm, R. M.   The effects of classroom instruction and discussion on death penalty opinions.   *Journal of Criminal Justice,* 1989, 17, 123-131.

Bohm, R. M.   Death penalty opinions.   *Sociological Inquiry,* 1990, 60, 285-297.

Bohm, R. M.   Retribution and capital punishment.   *Journal of Criminal Justice,* 1992, 20, 227-236.

Bohm, R. M., Clark, L. J., & Aveni, A. F.   The influence of knowledge on reasons for death penalty opinions.   *Justice Quarterly,* 1990, 7, 175-188.

Bohm, R. M., Clark, L. J., & Aveni, A. F.   Knowledge and death penalty opinion. *Journal of Research in Crime and Delinquency,* 1991, 28, 360-387.

Bohm, R. M., Flanagan, T. J., & Harris, P. W.   Current death penalty opinion in New York State.   *Albany Law Review,* 1990, 54, 819-843.

Bohm, R. M., & Vogel, R. E.   A comparison of factors associated with uninformed and informed death penalty opinions.   *Journal of Criminal Justice,* 1994, 22, 125-143.

Bohm, R. M., Vogel, R. E., & Maisto, A. A.   Knowledge and death penalty opinion. *Journal of Criminal Justice,* 1993, 21, 29-45.

Bowers, W. J.   Capital punishment and contemporary values.   *Law and Society Review,* 1993, 27(1), 157-175.

Bronson, E.   On the conviction proneness and representativeness of the death qualified jury.   *University of Colorado Law Review,* 1970, 42, 1-32.

Clagett, A. F., & Austin, S. F.   Relations of demographic characteristics to attitudes toward capital punishment.   *Quarterly Journal of Ideology,* 1986, 10(1), 48-53.

Claggett, W. J. M., & Shafer, B. E.   Life and death as public policy.   *International Journal of Public Opinion Research,* 1991, 3(1), 32-52.

Colman, A., & Gorman, P.   Conservatism, dogmatism, and authoritarianism in British police officers.   *Sociology,* 1982, 16(1), 1-11.

Combs, M., & Comer, J.   Race and capital punishment.   *Phylon,* 1982, 43, 350-359.

Cullen, F. T., Clark, G. A., Cullen, J., & Mathers, R. A.   Attribution, salience, and attitudes toward criminal sanctioning.   *Criminal Justice and Behavior,* 1985, 12, 305-331.

Curtis, J., & Lambert, R.   Education status and reactions to social and political heterogeneity.   *Canadian Review of Sociology and Anthropology,* 1976, 13, 189-203.

Curtis, J., & Perkins, K.   The capital punishment controversy.   *Journal of Humanics,* 1979, 7(1), 24-36.

Curtis, M. S. Attitudes toward the death penalty as it relates to political affiliation, religious beliefs, and faith in people. *Free Inquiry in Creative Sociology*, 1991, 19, 205-212.

Danigelis, N. L., & Cutler, S. J. Cohort trends in attitudes about law and order. *Public Opinion Quarterly*, 1991, 55(1), 24-49.

de Boer, C. The polls. *Public Opinion Quarterly*, 1979, 43, 410-418.

DeFronzo, J. In search of behavioral and attitudinal consequences of victimization. *Sociological Symposium*, 1979, 25, 23-29.

De Vries, B., & Walker, L. J. Moral reasoning and attitudes toward capital punishment. *Developmental Psychology*, 1986, 22, 509-513.

De Vries, B., & Walker, L. J. Conceptual/integrative complexity and attitudes toward capital punishment. *Personality and Social Psychology Bulletin*, 1987, 13, 448-457.

Ellsworth, P. C., & Gross, S. R. Hardening of the attitudes. *Journal of Social Issues*, 1994, 50(2), 19-52.

Ellsworth, P., & Ross, L. Public opinion and capital punishment. *Crime and Delinquency*, 1983, 29, 116-169.

Erskine, H. The polls. *Public Opinion Quarterly*, 1970, 34, 290-307.

Fagan, R. Police attitudes toward capital punishment. *Journal of Police Science and Administration*, 1986, 14, 193-201.

Feather, N. Factor structure of the conservatism scale. *Australian Psychologist*, 1975, 10, 179-184.

Finlay, B. Right to life vs. the right to die. *Sociology and Social Research*, 1985, 69, 548-560.

Fox, J. A., Radelet, M. L., & Bonsteel, J. L. Death penalty opinion in the post-*Furman* years. *New York Review of Law and Social Change*, 1990-1991, 18, 499-528.

Glenn, N. Recent trends in white-nonwhite attitudinal differences. *Public Opinion Quarterly*, 1974-1975, 38, 596-604.

Granberg, D., & Granberg, B. Pro-life versus pro-choice. *Sociology and Social Research*, 1981, 65, 424-434.

Grasmick, H. G., Cochran, J. K., Bursik, R. J., & Kimpel, M. Religion, punitive justice, and support for the death penalty. *Justice Quarterly*, 1993, 10, 289-314.

Hamm, M. S. Legislator ideology and capital punishment. *Justice Quarterly*, 1989, 6, 219-232.

Handberg, R., & Unkovic, C. M. Public opinion, the death penalty and the crime rate. *Free Inquiry in Creative Sociology*, 1985, 13, 141-144.

Harris, P. Over-simplification and error in public opinion surveys on capital punishment. *Justice Quarterly*, 1986, 3, 429-455.

Harvey, O. J. Belief systems and attitudes toward the death penalty and other punishments. *Journal of Personality*, 1986, 54, 659-675.

Holden, J. Demographics, attitudes, and afterlife beliefs of right-to-life and right-to-die organization members. *Journal of Social Psychology*, 1993, 133, 521-527.

Jepson, N. Homosexuality, capital punishment and the law. *British Journal of Delinquency*, 1959, 9, 246-257.

Johnson, G., & Newmeyer, J. Pleasure, punishment and moral indignation. *Sociology and Social Research*, 1975, 59, 82-95.

Jones, P. R. It's not what you ask, it's the way that you ask it. *Prison Journal*, 1994, 74, 32-50.

Jurow, G. New data on the effect of a "death qualified" jury on the guilt determination process. *Harvard Law Review*, 1971, 84, 567-611.

Keil, T. J., & Vito, G. F. Fear of crime and attitudes toward capital punishment. *Justice Quarterly*, 1991, 8, 447-464.

Kelley, J., & Braithwaite, J. Public opinion and the death penalty in Australia. *Justice Quarterly*, 1990, 7, 529-563.

Kohlberg, L., & Elfenbein, D. The development of moral judgements concerning capital punishment. *American Journal of Orthopsychiatry*, 1975, 45, 614-640.

Kristiansen, C. M., & Zanna, M. P. Value relevance and the value-attitude relation. *Basic and Applied Social Psychology*, 1991, 12, 471-483.

Larsen, K., Ommundsen, R., & Elder, R. Acquired immune deficiency syndrome. *Journal of Social Psychology*, 1991, 131, 289-291.

Larsen, K., Serra, M., & Long, E. AIDS victims and heterosexual attitudes. *Journal of Homosexuality*, 1990, 19(3), 103-116.

Lester, D. *Questions and answers about murder.* Philadelphia: Charles Press, 1991.

Lester, D., Hadley, R. A., & Lucas, W. A. Personality and a pro-death attitude. *Personality and Individual Differences*, 1990, 11, 1183-1185.

Lord, C., Ross, L., & Leper, M. Biased assimilation and attitude polarization. *Journal of Personality and Social Psychology*, 1979, 37, 2098-2109.

Lotz, R., & Regoli, R. Police, public and capital punishment. *Journal of Crime and Justice*, 1982, 5, 69-85.

McGarrell, E., & Sandys, M. The misperception of public opinion toward capital punishment. *American Behavioral Scientist*, 1996, 39, 500-513.

McKelvie, S. Personality and belief in capital punishment. *Personality and Individual Differences*, 1983, 4, 217-218.

McKelvie, S., & Daoussis, L. Extroversion and attitudes toward capital punishment. *Personality and Individual Differences*, 1982, 3, 341-342.

McShane, M. D., Williams, F. P., & Pelfrey, W. V. Eligibility for jury service in capital trials. *Texas Bar Journal*, 1987, 50, 365-370.

Midgley, J. Public opinion and the death penalty in South Africa. *British Journal of Criminology*, 1974, 14, 345-358.

Miller, A. G., McHoskey, J. W., Bane, C. M., & Dowd, T. G. The attitude polarization phenomenon. *Journal of Personality and Social Psychology*, 1993, 64, 561-574.

Mitchell, M., & Sidanius, J. Group status and ideological asymmetry. *National Journal of Sociology*, 1993, 7(1), 67-93.

Moran, G., & Comfort, J. C. Neither "tentative" nor "fragmentary." *Journal of Applied Psychology*, 1986, 71, 146-155.

Morsbach, H., & Morsbach, G. Attitudes toward capital punishment. *British Journal of Criminology*, 1967, 7, 394-403.

Moyser, G., & Medhurst, K. Political participation and attitudes in the Church of England. *Government Opposition*, 1978, 13(1), 81-95.

Musgrave, P., & Reid, G. Some measures of children's values. *Social Science Information*, 1971, 10, 137-153.

Neapolitan, J. Support for and opposition to capital punishment. *Criminal Justice and Behavior,* 1983, 10, 195-208.

Perkes, A., & Schildt, R. Death-related attitudes of adolescent males and females. *Death Education,* 1979, 2, 359-368.

Rankin, J. Changing attitudes toward capital punishment. *Social Forces,* 1979, 58, 194-211.

Ray, J. Attitudes to the death penalty in South Africa. *Journal of Social Psychology,* 1982, 116, 287-288.

Roberts, J. Public opinion and capital punishment. *Canadian Journal of Criminology,* 1984, 26, 283-291.

Ross, L. T., & Kaplan, K. J. Life ownership orientation and attitudes toward abortion, suicide, doctor-assisted suicide, and capital punishment. *Omega,* 1993-1994, 28, 17-30.

Ruggiero, J., & Weston, L. Comparative analysis of male and female attitudes. *International Journal of Sociology of the Family,* 1977, 7, 77-85.

Sandys, M., & McGarrell, E. F. Attitudes toward capital punishment among Indiana legislators. *Justice Quarterly,* 1994, 11, 651-677.

Sandys, M., & McGarrell, E. F. Attitudes toward capital punishment. *Journal of Research in Crime and Delinquency,* 1995, 32, 191-213.

Sarat, A., & Vidmar, N. Public opinion, the death penalty and the Eighth Amendment. *Wisconsin Law Review,* 1976, 171-206.

Sawyer, D. Public attitudes toward life and death. *Public Opinion Quarterly,* 1982, 46, 521-533.

Sebba, L., & Nathan, G. Further explorations in the scaling of penalties. *British Journal of Criminology,* 1984, 24, 221-249.

Seltzer, R., & McCormick, J. P. The impact of crime victimization and fear of crime on attitudes toward death penalty defendants. *Violence and Victims,* 1987, 2, 99-114.

Skovron, S. E., Scott, J. E., & Cullen, F. T. The death penalty for juveniles. *Crime and Delinquency,* 1989, 35, 546-561.

Smith, M. D. General versus specific support for capital punishment. *Journal of Crime and Justice,* 1987, 10(1), 117-132.

Smith, M. D., & Wright, J. Capital punishment and public opinion in the post-*Furman* era. *Sociological Spectrum,* 1992, 12, 127-144.

Smith, T. In search of house effects, *Public Opinion Quarterly,* 1978, 42, 443-463.

Snortum, J., & Ashear, V. Prejudice, punitiveness and personality. *Journal of Personality Assessment,* 1972, 36, 291-296.

Stamm, K., & Dube, R. The relationship of attitudinal components to trust in media. *Communications Research,* 1994, 21(1), 105-123.

Starr, J. Sex role orientation and attitudes toward institutional violence. *Humanity and Society,* 1983, 7, 127-148.

Stevens, D. J. The death sentence and inmate attitudes. *Crime and Delinquency,* 1992, 38, 272-279.

Stricker, G., & Jurow, G. The relationship between attitudes toward capital punishment and assignment of the death penalty. *Journal of Psychiatry and the Law,* 1974, 2, 415-422.

Swan, G. Gender, the judiciary and U.S. public opinion. *Journal of Social, Political and Economic Studies*, 1983, 8, 323-341.

Thayer, R. Attitudes and personality differences between potential jurors who could return a death verdict and those who could not. *Proceedings of the Annual Convention of the American Psychological Association*, 1970, 5(1), 445-446.

Thomas, C., & Foster, S. A sociological perspective on public support for capital punishment. *American Journal of Orthopsychiatry*, 1975, 45, 641-657.

Thomas, C., & Howard, R. Public attitudes toward capital punishment. *Journal of Behavioral Economics*, 1977, 6(1-2), 189-216.

Tygart, C. E. Respondents' "free will" view of criminal behavior and support for capital punishment. *International Journal of Public Opinion Research*, 1994, 6, 371-374.

Tyler, T., & Weber, R. Support for the death penalty. *Law and Society Review*, 1982, 17, 21-45.

Vidmar, N. Retributive and utilitarian motives and other correlates of Canadian attitudes toward the death penalty. *Canadian Psychologist*, 1974, 15, 337-356.

Warr, M. Public opinion on crime and justice. *Public Opinion Quarterly*, 1995, 59, 296-310.

Warr, M., & Stafford, M. Public goals of punishment and support for the death penalty. *Journal of Research in Crime and Delinquency*, 1984, 21, 95-111.

Watkins, D., & Sampson, J. Attitudes of Australian adolescents to crime and punishment. *Australian and New Zealand Journal of Sociology*, 1975, 11(2), 62-64.

Williams, F. P., Longmire, D. R., & Gulick, D. B. The public and the death penalty. *Criminal Justice Research Bulletin*, 1988, 3(8), 1-5.

Young, R. L. Race, conceptions of crime and justice, and support for the death penalty. *Social Psychology Quarterly*, 1991, 54, 67-75.

Young, R. L. Religious orientation, race and support for the death penalty. *Journal for the Scientific Study of Religion*, 1992, 31, 76-87.

Young, T. J., & French, L. A. Myths about aggression and attitudes about the death penalty. *Psychological Reports*, 1992, 71, 1337-1338.

Zeisel, H., & Gallup, A. M. Death penalty sentiment in the United States. *Journal of Quantitative Criminology*, 1989, 5, 285-296.

Chapter 7

DISCRIMINATION
AND THE DEATH PENALTY

One major argument against the use of the death penalty is that it was applied disproportionately more often to blacks than to whites. The research relevant to this issue will be reviewed in this chapter.

Early Studies

Johnson (1944) looked at murders in North Carolina in the 1930s. He found that the murderers of white victims were sentenced to death and life imprisonment more often than were the murderers of black victims. Black murderers of whites were executed more than other groups.

Garfinkel (1949) noted that blacks murdering whites were most likely to be executed for first-degree murder (37%) and whites killing blacks were least likely (0%).

Johnson (1957) studied convicted capital offenders in North Carolina from 1938 to 1953. He found that the probability of a death sentence and execution varied with the crime (murder versus rape, etc.), the motive for murder (gain versus passion), the race of the offender, and for rape the race and age of the victim.

In Texas from 1924 to 1968, Koeninger (1969) showed that blacks were less likely to get their death sentences commuted than were whites (16% versus 26%, respectively).

These early studies suffered from a major weakness. They failed to show that blacks and whites were committing similar types of murder. For example, blacks and whites might have differed in the weapons used for the murder, the motive for the murder, and so on. Later studies realized that many other factors might affect criminal justice system decisions about murder and sentencing, and these later studies sought to include a number of these variables in the analyses, including that of race.

Research Before 1984

Racial Discrimination for Cases of Murder

Judson et al. (1969) studied 238 first-degree murder sentencing decisions in California from 1958 to 1966. They found 67 variables which were related with the defendant receiving a death sentence. The variables covered such areas as the criminal's background, the victim's characteristics, the crime committed at the same time as the murder, and the circumstances of the trial. (Variables related to the attorneys were not related to the sentence.) The defendant's and victim's race were not, however, related to the sentence received.

Bowers and Pierce (1980) studied sentencing in four states under post-*Furman* statutes. They found that the probability of a death sentence was higher for blacks killing whites (for both felony and non-felony murders). The probability of a death sentence varied from state to state and between the different areas of each state. The racial difference showed up at all stages of the judicial process, from indictment to sentencing. In the appellate review, no effect of race was found in two states (Florida and Georgia).

Radelet (1981) studied homicide indictments in Florida in 1976 and 1977. The likelihood of a death sentence was higher for non-primary murder (that is, murder of a stranger) than for primary murder. For non-primary murders, the race of the murderer was not associated with a death sentence, but the race of the victim was (with white victims associated with a higher likelihood of a death sentence).

However, if the victim was white in a non-primary murder, the indictment was more likely to be for first-degree murder, but for first-degree murder indictments the race of the victim was not associated with a death sentence. Radelet concluded that discrimination was present only at the stage of choosing the indictment (first- versus second-degree murder, etc.).

Kleck (1981) studied the United States from 1931 to 1967. When he looked at the execution rate as a proportion of murder victims of the same race, he found that whites had the higher execution rates:

10.4 per 1,000 victims as compared to 9.7 for blacks. (Kleck noted that most murders were intraracial, and so the race of the victim is a fair approximation to the race of the offender). This difference was always true for non-Southern states and became true for Southern states after 1950.

Looking at death sentencing in the United States from 1967 to 1978, Kleck again found that non-whites had a lower risk of being sentenced to death (whether the proportion was calculated using the race of the victim or the race of the offender). For offenders, the risk of a death sentence was 13.4 for whites and 8.3 for non-whites.

Radelet and Vandiver (1983) looked at appeals of death sentences heard before the Florida Supreme Court from 1973 to 1981. For male defendants, 75 were affirmed (52%). Many variables were unrelated to the decision (whether the defendant was employed at the time of the crime, whether a plea bargain was offered, the original plea, the age of the victim and of the defendant, how the attorney was appointed, or the time between the trial and the Supreme Court decision). There were only eleven cases with black victims, so these cases were discarded. The Supreme Court decision was related to the jury recommendation and to the number of victims. In addition, white defendants with white female victims were the least likely to have their sentence overturned.

Paternoster (1984) studied 300 homicides with an accompanying felony in South Carolina from 1977 to 1981. (These were the most common form of murder for which a death sentence could be given.) The death penalty was sought by the prosecution in 107 of the cases. A death penalty was sought more often for some types of felonies, for white victims, if there were two or more felonies committed, if there were two or more victims, if there were two or more offenders, if the victim was female, if a gun was used for the murder, and if the victim was a stranger to the offender. (Age was not related to seeking a death sentence.) A death penalty was sought for 11 percent of black-kills-black murders, 37 percent of white-kills-white murders, 47 percent of white-kills-black murders and 49 percent of black-kills-white murders. Thus the racial factor was far from simple.

After the Furman Decision

Riedel (1976) compared sentencing outcomes before and after the *Furman* decision in 1972 which ruled that the death penalty was unconstitutional because it was imposed infrequently and with no clear standards. For the United States as a whole, a higher proportion of nonwhites was sentenced to death after *Furman* than before. This increase was most noteworthy in the Western states. (Little difference was found between states with a discretionary sentencing procedure and those with a mandatory procedure.)

Zeisel (1981) studied prisoners on death row in Florida during 1972 to 1977. He found that the vast majority of inmates had killed whites during a felony. For those killing whites, black defendants were more likely to be sentenced to death than white defendants. After the *Furman* decision in 1972, however, the percentage of blacks on death row dropped and the percentage of offenders who had killed blacks rose, thus suggesting that an effort was being made to reverse discriminatory biases that existed prior to the *Furman* decision.

Racial Discrimination in Rape Offenses

Wolfgang and Riedel (1973) noted that the proportion of blacks among those executed in the United States after 1930 for rape was greater than that for murder: 89 percent versus 55 percent. To explore this apparent discrimination in greater detail, they studied the imposition of the death penalty for rape in eleven Southern and border states from 1945 to 1965. In some 3,000 rape convictions, a death sentence was imposed on 13 percent of the blacks versus only 2 percent of the whites (a significant difference). For blacks raping white victims 36 percent received a death sentence, whereas for all other racial combinations only 2 percent received a death sentence. Various factors increased the likelihood of a death sentence, such as committing a contemporaneous offense along with the rape. They studied 24 such variables and found that racial differences existed even when these variables were taken into account.

In a study of rape convictions from 1945 to 1965, Wolfgang and Riedel (1975) found that the imposition of a death sentence was related to the race of the defendant and the victim (with black defendants and white victims being the most likely characteristics to result in a death sentence), the presence of a contemporaneous offense (which made it less likely that a death sentence would be imposed), and the year of the offense (with later years receiving fewer death sentences). No other variables related to the nature of the rape or to the trial were associated with the imposition of a death sentence.

Bowers (1974) presented data to show that blacks were executed more than whites for lesser crimes such as rape during the period of 1930 to 1970, at a younger age and with fewer appeals prior to execution. This discrimination was found more strongly in the South. For example, execution for rape was almost entirely a Southern phenomenon. Changing from mandatory to a discretionary death penalty had no effect on the racial discrimination, though the execution rate did go down after this switch in the laws.

Decision Making in the Criminal Justice System

Several studies have examined the factors affecting decisions about murderers in the criminal justice system.

Paternoster (1983) studied the decision by prosecutors to seek a death penalty in South Carolina from 1977 to 1981. He found that if a black killed a white, a death sentence was sought in 36 percent of the cases as compared to 13 percent for whites killing blacks. However, he noted that a greater proportion of the murders committed by blacks were capital cases under the death penalty statutes. Looking at only the capital murders, the prosecutor sought a death penalty at a high rate for all white victims and for whites killing blacks. For blacks killing blacks, the prosecutor was one-fourth as likely to seek a death penalty.

Paternoster found that the decision to seek a death penalty was associated also with the number of victims, the number of offenders, the gender of the victim, the weapon used, and the victim-offender relationship (but not with the age of the victim). The more of these factors present, the greater the likelihood that the prosecutor would ask for a death sentence.

The racial differential was found for most combinations of these other factors. For example, it was not found for multiple victims who were also strangers to the offender, but it was found for all other combinations.

In addition, the death sentence was sought more in some judicial circuits than in others (ranging from 2 percent to 28 percent of the capital murder cases in the different circuits). The probability was higher in rural court circuits than in urban circuits, even when the circumstances of the murder were the same.

Bowers (1983) looked at the indictment decisions in Florida from 1967 to 1977 for criminal homicide. The decision was related to whether the homicide was a felony-related killing, more than one offender, multiple victims, female victims, white victims, the region of the state and having a court-appointed attorney. Similarly, the likelihood of a first-degree murder conviction was related to some of these factors, including the race of the victim. However, the probability of a death sentence was related only to whether the killing was felony-related, the region of the state, and the type of attorney.

Baldus et al. (1983) found that, from 1973 to 1978 in Georgia, 17 percent of murder convictions resulted in a death sentence. The Georgia statute contains ten special circumstances about the murder, and Baldus found that the more of these special circumstances present, the greater the likelihood of a death sentence. This, therefore, seems appropriate.

Supreme Court Review

Looking at review decisions by the Georgia Supreme Court, Bowers (1983) found that the comparison cases chosen for reviewing a current case were not randomly selected from all possible 300 cases available but rather constituted a small selective sample.

Baldus et al. (1983) examined 68 cases reviewed by the Georgia Supreme Court by matching them with other cases for salient features. They found that the salient cases had a smaller proportion of death sentences. They concluded that the death sentence was being upheld in cases where comparable cases had a lower rate of death sentences, probably because the court did not use any cases receiving life sentences for comparison purposes. The Georgia Supreme Court rarely overturned a death sentence as being excessive punishment. However, Baldus noted that the court did overturn sentences on procedural grounds.

Commutations of Sentences

Bedau (1964) looked at death sentences in New Jersey from 1907 to 1960. Those commuted were more often females, non-felony murderers, offenders with no prior convictions, and younger offenders. Race, native-born, the sentencing power of the jury, whether the death penalty was mandatory or discretionary and whether the verdict was appealed were not significantly related to whether the sentence was commuted. (In a study of the period 1937 to 1961, the results were similar except that age was no longer related to commutation of the death sentence.) Bedau (1965) conducted a similar study on death sentences in Oregon, but presented no statistical tests of significance of the data.

Wolfgang et al. (1962) looked at prisoners sentenced to death in Pennsylvania from 1914 to 1958. Those who were executed (as compared to those whose sentences were commuted) were more likely to have committed felony murders and were more often aged 20 to 24 (but this was due to the higher incidence of felony murders in these men). For foreign-born whites, those committing felony murders were more likely to be executed than those committing non-felony murders. For native-born whites, the proportion executed was the same for felony and non-felony murders. For those committing felony murders, blacks were more likely to be executed. (The racial difference was not significant for non-felony murders.) Also, for blacks, those with court-appointed attorneys were more likely to be executed. Occupation and martial status were not related to commutation of the death sentence.

Is the Mandatory Death Penalty Mandatory?

Bedau (1976) studied murder in two counties in Massachusetts, focusing on cases of felony-murder-rape for which there was a mandatory death sentence. None of the 17 felony-murder-rapists received a death sentence, whereas two of the 111 murderers did. (Mostly, the felony-murder-rapists were convicted on lesser charges.) Thus, mandatory death sentencing turned out to be discretionary.

Discussion

Kleck (1981) reviewed studies on racial discrimination up to that point. For murder, three studies found racial discrimination in the death sentencing, five found no discrimination, and four studies produced mixed results. For rape, four studies found racial discrimination in the death sentencing while only one found no discrimination. Thus, racial discrimination seemed to be stronger for rape than for murder. In looking at non-capital punishment decisions, Kleck found that most studies reported evidence for discrimination. However, when controls for the prior record of the defendants were introduced, fewer studies reported discrimination. Thus, it is important to control for prior record and other variables in racial discrimination studies.

At first glance, therefore, it seems that blacks have been more severely treated with respect to capital punishment than have whites. (It is noteworthy that the severer treatment of males as compared to females has not attracted as much research interest.) However, it can also be seen that multivariate analyses of the decision-making process in the criminal justice system, from indictment, seeking a death sentence, the verdict, sentencing and review by superior courts have identified many variables relevant to these decisions. In some of these studies, race still appeared to be a relevant variable, even when other factors are taken into account. However, not all studies reported this racial effect.

Research in the Last Ten Years

Conviction and Sentencing

Ekland-Olson (1988) studied death sentences handed down in Texas from 1974 to 1983. Compared to murderers sentenced to prison sentences, death row inmates were more often white and had more often killed white victims. The race of the offender and victim was not associated with whether the death sentence was commuted or whether the death row inmate was actually executed.

Sorensen (1990) found that convictions for capital murder in Texas in post-*Furman* years was associated with legal factors (such as single versus multiple victims, rape plus homicide and stranger victims) and with extralegal factors such as the race of the victim. Once convicted, however, the sentence given was no longer associated with the race of the victim, only with legal factors such as single versus multiple victims and prior conviction record. In a report, apparently on these same data, Sorensen and Marquart (1990-1991) examined murderers in Texas from 1974 to 1988. Conviction for capital murder was associated with committing a felony rape and murder, not using gun, having a female victim, a white victim, a stranger as victim and multiple victims. Being sentenced to death was associated with knowing the victim, having multiple victims, having no co-defendants, not using a gun, have prior convictions, being a male offender, over the age of 25, being a professional, with higher education, and killing someone under the age of 20, female and white.

Vito and Keil (1988) looked at 458 capital cases in Kentucky from 1976 to 1986. One hundred and four cases had a death-qualified jury, and the probability of a death sentence was greater if the victim was white. In a multiple regression, the probability of a death sentence was greater if the murder was to prevent someone testifying. Vito and Keil next examined what predicted whether the prosecutor would seek a death-qualified jury. This was predicted by black offender/white victim and five circumstances of the crime (presence of a concurrent crime, murder to silence the victim, more than one murder, a female victim, and multiple aggravating circumstances).

Keil and Vito (1989) reported on 407 men convicted for murder in Kentucky from 1977 to 1986, cases which presumably overlap with those in the previous report. Those tried before a death-qualified jury more often had multiple victims, to be blacks killing whites and to have committed more "serious" murders (that is, deliberate and heinous murder of strangers). Those sentenced to death were more likely to have multiple victims, female victims and white victims and to have committed more serious murders. Prior convictions for violent crime did not predict a death sentence.

Keil and Vito (1990) again reported on murder trials in Kentucky from 1976 to 1986. Capital charges and death sentences were most common for blacks killing whites and least for whites killing blacks. Capital charges and death sentences were associated with multiple victims, the victim silenced, a history of violent offenses, multiple aggravating circumstances, and blacks killing whites. However, Keil and Vito looked only at the bivariate correlations and did not explore a multiple regression analysis to see which factors were the strongest predictors of a death sentence. In a later study, Keil and Vito (1992) found that the percentage of blacks executed in the Southern states decreased after the *Gregg* decision from the Supreme Court in 1976.

Radelet and Pierce (1985) studied murder defendants in Florida from 1973 to 1977. For the felony murders, the probability of a death sentence was higher if the victim was white and if the case was upgraded to a felony murder and there was no plea bargaining. If the victim was white, there was a reduced probability of plea bargaining. The probability of a death sentence was predicted by upgrading the case to felony murder and the number of victims but not by the offender's race, the number of offenders, the victim's or offender's gender, the weapon used or whether the victim was a stranger.

Radelet and Pierce (1991) studied death sentences handed down in Florida in a later period, from 1976 to 1987, and found that white defendants and murders with white victims were more often sentenced to death than were black defendants and murders with black victims. However, blacks killing whites were most often sentenced to death. A large number of other variables predicted the probability of a death sentence: felony murder, the number of victims, the number of offenders, the victim's gender and relationship to the murderer, and the location (urban/rural).

Foley (1987) examined first-degree murder cases in 21 of Florida's counties for 1972 to 1978. The imposition of a death sentence was predicted by male offender, white victim, multiple victims, additional offenses, felony murder and the county (but not significantly with the race of the offender, the gender of the victim, accomplices, relationship to victim, weapon, age of offender or type of attorney).

Heilbrun et al. (1989) studied 243 men convicted of murder in Georgia from 1974 to 1987 and given the death sentence or life imprisonment. Those receiving the death penalty were more likely to be blacks killing whites and to be more dangerous (which was defined as having an antisocial personality disorder and a low intelligence test score). However, controlling for dangerousness (the black murderers were more dangerous than the white murderers), Heilbrun found that whites were more likely to be given a death sentence at all levels of dangerousness (except for the most dangerous where 100 percent of both whites and blacks were given a death sentence). Thus, there was no racial bias in these sentences.

Bohm (1994) claimed to find evidence for racial discrimination in Georgia, but his data in fact show "reverse" racism. In a poorly designed study with no statistical analysis of the data, Bohm claimed to look at two judicial circuits in Georgia from 1973-1990. In fact, he examines data from one or the other (but rarely both) or from the whole state of Georgia, for varying time periods, with varying definitions of his variables (such as sometimes studying blacks and sometimes non-whites). The percentage of non-white murderers in Georgia in 1989 was reported to be 64 percent, the percentage of black defendants in capital cases from 1973 to 1990 in the two judicial circuits was reported to be 62 percent, and the percentage of executed murderers who were black in the two judicial circuits post-*Furman* was 67 percent. These percentages seem quite similar.

In one judicial circuit, Bohm claimed that murders with white victims were more often capital cases if the murder was accompanied by a felony, for stranger and non-stranger victims, for male and female victims and for single (but not multiple) victims. However, Bohm did not carry out a multiple regression analysis to test the statistical significance of this set of variables.

Bohm reported that the population was 56% white in one circuit. Jurors for murder trials were 65% white, but when the defendant was white, only 52% of the jurors were white while when the defendant was black 69% of the jurors were white. Thus, it appears that white murderers were tried by juries that had a higher percentage of blacks than did black murderers. Furthermore, jurors who were struck from the jury were more often white if the murderer was white.

Finally, Bohm noted that the judges and district attorneys in the two counties were all white, and 97% of the lawyers were white.

Ralph et al. (1992) examined murderers convicted in Texas from 1923 to 1971. Those sentenced to death were younger than those imprisoned, but did not differ in race or the region of Texas where the trial was held. Limiting the sample to 1942 to 1971, Ralph found that those sentenced to death were more often professionals, more educated, had more often served time in prison, had more co-defendants, more often killed multiple, female and stranger victims, had more often committed a felony murder, were more often white offenders, had more often killed white victims, and more often were non-whites killing whites. A multiple regression, however, found that only felony murder, prior prison time, white offender, white victim and female victim predicted a death sentence.

Bienen et al. (1988) examined all homicides in New Jersey from 1982 to 1988. On the 703 cases, 25 were sentenced to death. The percentage of blacks at the various stages were as follows: all homicides (56.6%), death sentence possible (57.4%), death sentence eligible (57.3%), capital murder trial (56.4%), penalty phases (53.6%) and death sentence imposed (56.0%). It can be seen that these percentages stayed roughly the same at the various phases. Death sentences were imposed more often for white victims (9.9%) than for black victims (3.6%), but the race of the murderer when the victim was white favored whites receiving a death sentence (10.6% for whites murdering whites and 8.2% for blacks murdering whites).

Murphy (1984) examined felony murders in Cook County (OH) from 1977 to 1981 and found that white victims resulted in death sentences most often. However, Murphy examined the impact only of race and did not study the role of other factors in this decision.

Smith (1987) examined homicides in Los Angeles from 1976 to 1982. The probability of a death sentence was greater for white victims and female victims, but was not related to the defendant's race, number of victims, the weapon used or the victim-murderer relationship.

Baldus et al. (1985) examined homicides in Georgia from 1979 to 1981 and found that a death sentence was more likely for white victims, aggravating circumstances, female victims, young victims, a bloody murder, a police officer or fireman victim, a stranger victim and multiple victims and less likely for mitigating circumstances, a high-status defendant, and being an accessory. Post-*Furman*, the race of the defendant was not statistically significant overall, not statistically significant in rural areas, but biased against whites in urban areas.

Gross and Mauro (1984) found that death sentences in Georgia, Florida and Illinois were more likely if the murder was a felony homicide, with a victim who was a white, stranger or female, multiple victims, did not use gun, in rural areas, with aggravating circumstance, and in Georgia and Florida as compared to Illinois. The race of the victim was statistically significant in a multiple regression analysis which controlled for the other variables. A study of Georgia and Florida found that the race of the victim was still important in the appellate review. In less rigorous analyses, the impact of the race of the victim was statistically significant in Oklahoma, Mississippi, and North Carolina but not in Arkansas or Virginia.

Barnett (1985) examined homicides in Georgia from 1973 to 1978. He found that a deliberate murder, the victim-murderer relationship and the heinousness of the killing affected the probability of receiving a death sentence. The death sentence rate was also higher in rural regions, if the defendant had a prior criminal record, and for white victims for some patterns on murder based on Barnett's three major variables (deliberateness, relationship and heinousness). The effect of race also depended on the other variables. For example, the death sentence rate for blacks killing whites was higher if the defendant had prior convictions; but the death sentence rate for whites killing whites was higher if the defendant had no prior convictions.

The Decision to Seek the Death Penalty

Berk et al. (1993) examined homicides in San Francisco County in 1978 to 1988 and found that 7.4 percent were charged with special circumstances so that the death penalty applied. Of seventy explanatory variables, the significant predictors of such a charge were white offender, female victim, the number of prior felonies, the number of prior homicides, the number of victims, and whether the victim and murderer were strangers.

Baldus et al. (1986) studied 179 death-eligible cases in Colorado from 1980 to 1984. Not all were charged with capital murder, others plea bargained, and some were found not guilty. Only eleven faced the death penalty and only four received it. Thus, a death sentence was quite rare.

Kazyaka (1990) studied 299 homicides in South Carolina from 1977 to 1981 and found that the prosecution sought the death penalty more often if a black killed a white and less often if a black killed a black. Appellate review of the convictions did not change this bias.

Paternoster and Kazyaka (1988) reported on 302 felony homicides in South Carolina from 1977 to 1981, apparently the same cases as in the report above. The prosecutor was more likely to seek the death penalty if the victim was white, there were multiple victims, the victim was a stranger, the defendant had prior convictions, used a gun and there were aggravating factors. In the multiple regression, only the last three factors were statistically significant. There were differences in these results if the urban and rural regions of the state were considered separately, with race playing a stronger role in rural regions.

The death sentence was imposed more often for white defendants, black victims, and for whites killing blacks. Other predictive variables included the number of victims, the number of offenders, and the mitigating and aggravating circumstances. Affirmations of the death sentence by the South Carolina Supreme Court were predicted by similar variables.

A later study of South Carolina from 1979 to 1987 (Paternoster & Kazyaka, 1989-1990) found that affirmation of the death sentence by the state supreme court was predicted by the number of offenders, the race of the offender, the brutality of the murder, the number of felonies, and the use of a handgun. The race of the victim and the mitigating circumstances had only a very weak role. Paternoster and Kazyaka found that some types of cases were nearly always affirmed, indicating that a death sentence was typical for these cases; other types of cases were rarely affirmed indicating that a death sentence was rare and possibly arbitrary.

Bienen et al. (1990) studied 146 felony murders in New Jersey from 1982 to 1988. Of the 146 cases, only 15 received a death sentence. The decision to go to trial was more likely if the victim was white, but the decision to make the case eligible was more likely if the victim was Hispanic. Thereafter, the victim's and defendant's race did not predict the decision. (Bienen also found differences in the decision to go to trial and to make the case death eligible from county to county.)

Bienen et al. carried out a regression analysis for predicting "death possible" cases (the prosecutor decides to serve a notice of factors). The variables which significantly predicted this decision were the county, the victim's race, the presence of aggravating and mitigating circumstances and the some of the circumstances of the case.

Executions

Radelet (1989) studied the Espy files of executions in America from 1608 to the present time. Looking at executions of whites for killing blacks, Radelet found only 26 cases (with 30 defendants) in 15,978 executions. All 30 offenders were male, and 23 of the victims were male. Ten cases involved murdering slaves (including two slave owners), in seven cases the defendant had prior criminal convictions, in five cases the black victim was of higher social status than the white murderer (for example, a black employer murdered by a white employee), in four cases the murderer was of extremely low social class ("white trash"), and in four cases the crime was heinous.

Aguirre and Baker (1989) noted that 773 prisoners were executed in Arizona, California, Colorado, New Mexico and Texas from 1890 to 1986. Of these, 14 percent were Mexican Americans which approximates their percentage in the population in these states. However, Aguirre and Baker noted that the Mexican Americans who were executed were less likely to appeal their convictions to higher courts.

Phillips (1986) studied 261 counties in Georgia and North Carolina from 1925 to 1935, comparing counties where rate of executions for black offenders was greater than that for white offenders with those where it was less. The rate of executions for black offenders was greater in counties which were more urban and in North Carolina, with a greater percentage of blacks, a higher lynching rate, and more economic and educational discrimination. Beck et al. (1989) found a positive association between the execution rate and the lynching rate for blacks in North Carolina and Georgia from 1822 to 1930, supporting a conflict model rather than a substitution model for explaining lynchings.

Women and the Death Penalty

Rapaport (1991) noted that although women committed 14.3 percent of murders and non-negligent manslaughters in America from 1976 to 1987, they committed only 6.2 percent of the felony murders and 3.9 percent of the murders of strangers. Thus, their representation on death row should be compared with an expected percentage of around 4 percent rather than 14 percent.

Rapaport compared 39 women sentenced to death in America from 1978 to 1987 with 84 men sentenced to death in North Carolina from 1977 to 1989. The men had more prior convictions for violent felonies, but did not differ in the incidence of felony murder or multiple victims.

Rape

Grimes (1994) studied 1,339 rape convictions from 1945 to 1965 in six Southern states where rape was still a capital offense. Race was the dominant predictor of a death sentence, but other factors played a role (such as urban/rural location, legal and prosecutorial procedures, the nature and the circumstances of the rape, and non-racial characteristics of the victim and the offender).

Hunter et al. (1993) studied rapists sentenced to death from 1942 to 1971 in Texas and found that those sentenced to death were more often black, slightly younger, more often from Houston and Dallas, with more prior arrests, more often using weapons, more often raping outdoors (rather than in homes or cars), with older victims, stranger victims, and white victims. However, Hunter did not carry out a multiple regression to see which of these predictor variables survived a multivariate analysis.

Judges Versus Juries

Radelet (1985) studied capital murder cases in Florida from 1972 to 1984. He found that juries were less likely to impose the death penalty than were judges. The imposition of the death penalty by juries was predicted by few of the variables examined, except that having a private attorney was associated with a lesser probability of a death sentence.

Appellate Review

Radelet and Vandiver (1983) compared death penalties affirmed by the Florida Supreme Court and those not affirmed from 1973 to 1981. Affirmation was predicted by the jury recommendation and by having multiple victims. If the victim was male, white offenders were more likely to have the death penalty affirmed; if the victim was female, black offenders were more likely to have the death penalty affirmed. The type of attorney played no role in affirmation.

Hall and Brace (1994) looked at Supreme Court votes in six states during the 1980s and found that justices voting in favor of the death penalty were more likely to be Republicans, with prosecutorial backgrounds and older (over 61 years of age). Justices voted in favor of the death penalty more for female victims, elderly victims, for killing police officers, and if rape was involved in the murder.

Discussion

Recent research on discrimination and the death penalty has focused more on death sentences than on executions. The studies on sentencing have produced mixed results. Seven studies found that murderers of white victims were more likely to be sentenced to death than murderers of black victims; however, five studies found that white murderers were more likely to be sentenced to death than black murderers, with three of these studies also finding that white victims increased the probability of a death sentence. One study found mixed results, while another found that murderers of black victims were more likely to be sentenced to death. The preponderance of the evidence seems to suggest that killing a white victim may be more likely to result in a death sentence than killing a black victim, though this bias is no longer as clear as it once was.

The two studies of executions, however, found no racial bias. Thus, it would appear that the racial bias in capital punishment is much less than in earlier years and may be disappearing completely.

Interestingly, very little research has been conducted on the other bias in capital punishment, the differential sentencing and execution of men and women, a topic that appears to arouse less interest among researchers than racial bias.

REFERENCES

Aguirre, A., & Baker, D. The execution of Mexican-American prisoners in the Southwest. *Social Justice*, 1989, 16, 150-161.

Baldus, D. C., Pulaski, C. A., & Woodworth, G. Comparative review of death sentences. *Journal of Criminal Law and Criminology*, 1983, 74, 661-753.

Baldus, D. C., Pulaski, C. A., & Woodworth, G. Arbitrariness, and discrimination in the administration of the death penalty. *Stetson Law Review*, 1986, 15, 133-261.

Baldus, D. C., Woodworth, G., & Pulaski, C. A. Monitoring and evaluating contemporary death sentencing systems. *University of California Davis Law Review*, 1985, 18, 1375-1407.

Barnett, A. Some distribution patterns for the Georgia death sentence. *University of California Davis Law Review*, 1985, 18, 1327-1374.

Beck, E. M., Massey, J. L., & Tolnay, S. E. The gallows, the mob, and the vote. *Law and Society Review*, 1989, 23, 317-331.

Bedau, H. Death sentences in New Jersey 1907-1960. *Rutgers Law Review*, 1964, 19, 1-64.

Bedau, H. Capital punishment in Oregon. *Oregon Law Review*, 1965, 45, 1-39.

Bedau, H. Felony murder rape and the mandatory death penalty. *Suffolk University Law Review*, 1976, 10, 493-520.

Berk, R. A., Boger, J., & Weiss, R. Chance and the death penalty. *Law and Society Review*, 1993, 27(1), 89-110.

Bienen, L. B., Weiner, N. A., Allison, P. D., & Mills, D. L. The reimposition of capital punishment in New Jersey. *Albany Law Review*, 1990, 54, 709-817.

Bienen, L. B., Weiner, N. A., Denno, D. W., Allison, P. D., & Mills, D. L. The reimposition of capital punishment in New Jersey. *Rutgers Law Review*, 1988, 41, 27-327.

Bohm, R. M. Capital punishment in two judicial circuits in Georgia. *Law and Human Behavior*, 1994, 18, 319-338.

Bowers, W. *Executions in America.* Lexington: D. C. Heath, 1974.

Bowers, W. The pervasiveness of arbitrariness and discrimination under post-*Furman* capital statutes. *Journal of Criminal Law and Criminology*, 1983, 74, 1067-1100.

Bowers, W., & Pierce, G. Arbitrariness and the discrimination under post-*Furman* capital statutes. *Crime and Delinquency*, 1980, 26, 563-635.

Ekland-Olson, S. Structured discretion, racial bias, and the death penalty. *Social Science Quarterly*, 1988, 69, 853-873.

Foley, L. A. Florida after the *Furman* decision. *Behavioral Sciences and the Law*, 1987, 5, 457-465.

Garfinkel, H. Research note on inter- and intra-racial homicides. *Social Forces*, 1949, 27, 369-381.

Grimes, R. E. M. J. Rape, race, and the death penalty revisited. *Dissertation Abstracts International*, 1994, 54A, 3601.

Gross, S. R., & Mauro, R. Patterns of death. *Stanford Law Review*, 1984, 37, 27-153.

Hall, M. G., & Brace, P. The vicissitudes of death by decree. *Social Science Quarterly*, 1994, 75, 136-151.

Heilbrun, A. B., Foster, A., & Golden, J. The death sentence in Georgia, 1974-1987. *Criminal Justice and Behavior*, 1989, 16, 139-154.

Hunter, R. J., Ralph, P. H., & Marquart, J. The death sentencing of rapists in pre-*Furman* Texas (1942-1971). *American Journal of Criminal Law*, 1993, 20, 313-337.

Johnson, E. Selective factors in capital punishment. *Social Forces*, 1957, 36, 165-169.

Johnson, G. The negro and crime. *Annals of the American Academy of Political and Social Science*, 1941, #217, 93-104.

Judson, C., Pondell, J., Owens, J., McIntosh, J., & Matschullat, D. A study of the California penalty jury in first-degree murder cases. *Stanford Law Review*, 1969, 21, 1297-1497.

Kazyaka, A. M. Guarding the gateway to discrimination. *Dissertation Abstracts International*, 1990, 50A, 4111.

Keil, T. J., & Vito, G. F. Race, homicide severity, and the application of the death penalty. *Criminology*, 1989, 27, 511-535.

Keil, T. J., & Vito, G. F. Race and the death penalty in Kentucky murder trials. *Justice Quarterly*, 1990, 7, 189-207.

Keil, T. J., & Vito, G. F. The effects of the *Furman* and *Gregg* decisions on black-white execution ratios in the South. *Journal of Criminal Justice*, 1992, 20, 217-226.

Kleck, G. Racial discrimination in criminal sentencing. *American Sociological Review*, 1981, 46, 783-805.

Koeninger, R. Capital punishment in Texas 1924-1968. *Crime and Delinquency*, 1969, 15, 132-141.

Paternoster, R. Race of victim and location of crime. *Journal of Criminal Law and Criminology*, 1983, 74, 754-785.

Paternoster, R. Prosecutorial discretion in requesting the death penalty. *Law and Society Review*, 1984, 18, 437-478.

Paternoster, R., & Kazyaka, A. M. The administration of the death penalty in South Carolina. *South Carolina Law Review*, 1988, 39, 245-411.

Paternoster, R., & Kazyaka, A. M. An examination of comparatively excessive death sentences in South Carolina 1979-1987. *New York University Review of Law and Social Change*, 1989-1990, 17, 475-533.

Phillips, C. D. Social structure and social control. *Social Forces*, 1986, 65, 458-475.

Radelet, M. L. Racial characteristics and the imposition of the death penalty. *American Sociological Review*, 1981, 46, 918-927.

Radelet, M. L. Executions of whites for crimes against blacks. *Sociological Quarterly*, 1989, 30, 529-544.

Radelet, M. L. Rejecting the jury. *University of California Davis Law Review*, 1985, 18, 1409-1431.

Radelet, M. L., & Pierce, G. L. Race and prosecutorial discretion in homicide cases. *Law and Society Review*, 1985, 19, 587-621.

Radelet, M. L., & Pierce, G. L. Choosing those who will die. *Florida Law Review*, 1991, 43, 1-34.

Radelet, M. L., & Vandiver, M. The Florida Supreme Court and death penalty appeals. *Journal of Criminal Law and Criminology*, 1983, 74, 913-926.

Ralph, P. H., Sorensen, J. R., & Marquart, J. W. A comparison of death-sentenced and incarcerated murderers in pre-*Furman* Texas. *Justice Quarterly*, 1992, 9, 185-209.

Rapaport, E. The death penalty and gender discrimination. *Law and Society Review*, 1991, 25, 367-383.

Riedel, M. Discrimination in the imposition of the death penalty. *Temple Law Quarterly*, 1976, 49, 261-287.

Smith, M. D. Patterns of discrimination in assessments of the death penalty. *Journal of Criminal Justice*, 1987, 15, 279-286.

Sorensen, J. R. The effects of legal and extralegal factors on prosecutorial and jury decision-making in post-*Furman* Texas capital cases. *Dissertation Abstracts International*, 1990, 51A, 1398.

Sorensen, J. R., & Marquart, J. W. Prosecutorial and jury decision-making in post-*Furman* Texas capital cases. *New York University Review of Law and Social Change*, 1990-1991, 18, 743-776.

Vito, G. F., & Keil, T. J. Capital sentencing in Kentucky. *Journal of Criminal Law and Criminology*, 1988, 79, 483-503.

Wolfgang, M., & Riedel, M. Race, judicial discretion and the death penalty. *Annals of the American Academy of Political and Social Science*, 1973, #407, 119-133.

Wolfgang, M., & Riedel, M. Rape, race and the death penalty in Georgia. *American Journal of Orthopsychiatry*, 1975, 45, 658-668.

Wolfgang, M., Kelly, A., & Noble, H. Comparison of the executed and the commuted along admissions to death row. *Journal of Criminal Law, Criminology and Police Science*, 1962, 53, 301-311.

Zeisel, H. Race bias in the administration of the death penalty. *Harvard Law Review*, 1981, 95, 456-468.

Chapter 8

JURIES AND THE DEATH PENALTY

Some research has been conducted on how juries might respond to cases involving murder and other crimes, and the research is reviewed in this chapter.

Does a Death Sentence Deter a Guilty Verdict?

Hester and Smith (1973) had students read a trial in which the defendant, if found guilty, would be given a death sentence or life imprisonment. If the sentence was to be a death sentence, they were less likely to find the defendant guilty. This effect was significant for a gang-war murder case, but not for a heinous murder of a child.

Haney (1984) selected potential jurors who were moderates, that is, who would consider a death sentence in some cases and who would not let a possible death sentence change their impartiality. They were shown a videotape of a jury selection procedure (but not trial!). Some were shown a tape with a death-qualification section and some were shown a tape without this section. Those shown the death-qualification section were more likely to see the defendant as guilty and to see a death sentence as appropriate if the defendant were to be found guilty.

Freedman (1990) questioned jurors who served on juries for first-degree murder trials in Canada where there was no death penalty. Thirty percent said that they would have been less likely to convict the offender had there been a death penalty compared to only three percent who said that they would have been more likely to convict.

The Effect of the Crime and its Commission

Hendrick and Shaffer (1975) had college students read a brief account of a murder trial. When asked if they were in favor of a death penalty for the murderer, the number of murderers (one murderer versus five) had no impact. However, if the victim was mutilated, then the students were more in favor of a death penalty (and more punitive in allocating a term of imprisonment).

Finkel and Smith (1993) presented college students and community residents with cases of murder and found that they were less likely to convict and sentence offenders who served as accessories to felony murders to death than the actual killer. The type of accessory also played a role in these decisions, such as a getaway driver versus a more active participant, and, if the accessory was tried at the same time as the killer, then conviction and a death sentence were less likely than if the accessory was tried alone. Finkel and Duff (1991) found similar results when college students played the role of jurors and justices deciding whether to let the jury decision stand. They also found that the mode of death of the victim played a role (such as dying from a heart attack during a robbery, dying from a firearm discharging accidentally, dying in a brutal fashion or dying because of premeditation).

Assigning the Death Penalty

Hamilton and Rotkin (1979) gave people vignettes of crimes and asked them to assign a sentence. The assignment of a death sentence was not associated with the offender's race (in three of the four vignettes; in the fourth, whites received a death sentence more than blacks), whether the killing was victim-precipitated, or whether the killer had been hired to kill. If the murderer had a low intelligence test score, for white offenders this decreased the likelihood of a death sentence, whereas for black offenders it increased the likelihood.

Ellsworth and Ross (1983) asked people how much evidence they would want if serving on a jury. Respondents wanted more evidence before imposing a death sentence than before imposing life imprisonment.

Finkel et al. (1994) gave college students who met the criteria for death-qualification juries cases to read and had them assign sentences. They found that heinous murders and the type of defendant (principal versus accessory) had an impact on the proportion of death sentences assigned, as did the age of the murderer. On the whole, younger murderers were less often sentenced to death, but there were non-linearities in the results, which Finkel passed over in his discussion of the study.

White (1987) found that college students pretending to be jurors were more likely to sentence the defendant to death if he had killed many victims than if he had murdered while committing a robbery. The students sentenced the defendant to death more often when the defense used a mental illness defense than when the defense presented conceptual arguments against the death penalty. Other factors affecting the sentence were the defendant's volition and the jurors' view of his future dangerousness. The gender of the juror had no impact on the sentence.

Effect of Favoring the Death Penalty on Verdicts

Gleason and Harris (1976) found that students participating in mock juries judging an armed robber found him more guilty, more blameworthy and as less similar to themselves if they favored capital punishment.

Jurow (1971) had people listen to tapes of two cases (armed robbery and rape). Those favoring capital punishment were more likely to find the robber guilty, but did not differ on the verdict in the rape case.

Bernard and Dwyer (1984) found that juries composed of students with differing attitudes toward capital punishment came to decisions about guilt quite easily and that the choices of the individual jurors were not related to their attitudes toward the death penalty. However, the juries had difficulty coming to a decision about the sentence. Individual attitudes toward capital punishment clearly affected the decision to sentence the murderer to death, and deliberation in the jury did not change these individual decisions.

Moran and Comfort (1986) studied jurors who had served on juries at felony trials. Jurors who favored capital punishment were more likely to favor conviction before deliberating (this was true for only female jurors), but their attitude toward capital punishment did not affect their final verdict.

Luginbuhl and Middendorf (1988) found that prospective jurors were more in favor of the death penalty if they were white, male, older and less educated. Their attitudes toward the death penalty was not associated with their willingness to take aggravating circumstances (such as killing for monetary gain) into account. However, those opposed to the death penalty considered the mitigating circumstances (such as the offender is a juvenile) more important.

Death-Qualified Jurors

Witherspoon v. Illinois (391 US 510 [1968]) permitted the exclusion of jurors on capital murder cases if they were unwilling to impose a death penalty or if they were unwilling to find the defendant guilty if a death sentence was possible. Several studies have appeared looking at differences between jurors who are death-qualified and those who are excludable on these (and other) criteria.[1]

Fitzgerald and Ellsworth (1984) surveyed potential jurors and found that death-qualified jurors were, of course, more in favor of capital punishment. They were also more punitive, more concerned with crime control than due process, favored the prosecution more, and mistrusted the defendant and his attorney more. Death-qualified jurors were more often male, white, Protestants or Catholics, wealthy, and Republicans. (They did not differ in education or in being self-employed.)

Ellsworth et al. (1984) found that death-qualified potential jurors were less likely to accept an insanity defense for schizophrenic defendants in cases presented to them, but were as likely to find those with organic diseases not guilty through reason of insanity as excludable jurors.

Cowan et al. (1984) had potential jurors watch a murder trial and found that death-qualified jurors were more likely to find the defendant guilty. Death-qualified jurors were also more likely to be male and non-Catholics. They did not differ in race, marital status, education or political affiliation. Death-qualified jurors did not differ in their recall of the evidence presented or in the judge's instructions. Overall, the verdict given was unrelated to age, sex, education, or previous jury experience, but the verdict was related to attitudes toward the death penalty. Juries composed solely of death-qualified jurors had worse recall of the evidence than mixed juries but did not differ in their recall of the judge's instructions.

---

1. A different set of criteria for excluding jurors was proposed in *Wainwright v. Witt* (53 LW 4108 [1985]).

Thompson et al. (1984) showed potential jurors a videotape of an assault trial (by a black man on a white police officer). Those who were death-qualified favored the prosecution's case more than excludable jurors did. In situations in which an innocent man was convicted and a guilty man found innocent, the death-qualified jurors showed less regret for the erroneous conviction and more regret for the erroneous acquittal.

Cox and Tanford (1989) studied college students who were opposed to the death penalty and were excludable using the *Witherspoon* criterion. When these students were given sixteen actual scenarios involving murder, 65 percent of them would favor the death penalty for at least one of the scenarios. Thus, their general opposition to the death penalty did not translate into opposition in every particular situation. These students who showed this inconsistency were less punitive and more due-process oriented than the death-qualified students.

Similarly, Robinson (1993) found that, while death-qualified jurors (based on the *Witherspoon* criteria but who said they would fairly follow the judges' instructions) would be more likely to consider the death penalty for five murder cases which he presented to them, the non-qualified jurors were not unanimously opposed to the death penalty—indeed 60 percent of the excludables indicated that they would be prepared to go along with the death penalty on at least one of the five cases with which they were presented. Robinson argued that it was not necessary, therefore, to exclude all jurors who failed to meet the *Witherspoon* criteria.

Williams and McShane (1990) studied community residents in Texas. They were given vignettes of capital cases, their attitudes toward capital punishment assessed and their jury eligibility examined. Using the *Witherspoon* criteria, the excludables and non-excludables did not differ in whether they would vote for conviction. Regarding imposing a death penalty, white male jurors were more likely to vote yes, while white defendants were less likely to be sentenced to death by minority "jurors."

Nieses and Dillehay (1987) studied a sample of registered voters in one Kentucky county and found that 77 percent favored the death penalty. The *Witt* standard for excluding jurors excluded more than the *Witherspoon* criteria (21% versus 14%). The *Witt* excludables were less opposed to the death penalty than the *Witherspoon* excludables and less due process oriented. Females were more often excludable than males.

Seltzer and McCormick (1987) found that the associations between death penalty attitude items was different for death-qualified people than for those not qualified.

Elliott and Robinson (1991) had college students watch a trial in groups. They found that those who were *Witherspoon* excludables were no less likely to give guilty verdicts than the death-qualified students. The nullifiers (those who said that they could not be fair and impartial) were more likely to vote for acquittal.

Haney et al. (1994) examined a group of Californian residents, comparing those who were excludable with those who were not using both the *Witt* and *Witherspoon* criteria. The excludables had different attitudes toward criminal justice issues and the death penalty, as expected, and they also differed in how they took into account mitigating and aggravating circumstances–the excludables gave mitigating circumstances more weight and aggravating circumstances less weight.

Horowitz and Seguin (1986) took prospective jurors and compared their judgments on hypothetical cases depending on whether they were death-qualified or not and on whether they decided both guilt and the sentence or only one of these two decisions. The death-qualified bifurcated juries rendered a verdict of guilt more often and gave more severe sentences.

Seltzer et al. (1987) found that death-qualified jurors differed in attitudes toward criminal justice as compared to those who were not death-qualified. For example, more of the former agreed that the courts were too lenient, and they seemed to be more conviction prone.

McShane et al. (1987) reported that those eligible for jury duty in capital trials in Texas were more often male, white, upper income, opposed to rehabilitation for criminals and in favor of retribution. McShane found that their excludables included those who would automatically impose the death penalty (3%), those who were totally opposed (15%), and those who refused to serve (12%).

The Process of Jury Selection

Nietzel et al. (1987) examined trials in California, Kentucky and South Carolina, comparing those in which the prospective jurors were interviewed alone and those in which they were interviewed en masse.

For jurors interviewed alone, more were removed as a result of defense-inspired challenges, but there were no differences in *Witherspoon*-based challenges or prosecution-inspired challenges. Nietzel also found that imposition of a death sentence was not significantly associated with the method for interviewing jurors, nor with the use of jury consultants.

Judges' Instructions

Luginbuhl (1992) took people who were on jury lists and had them listen to two versions of judge's instructions for the penalty phase of a trial. The people's understanding of the legal issues differed for the two versions, indicating that the judge's instructions are critical in this respect.

Haney and Lynch (1994) read undergraduates the California judicial instructions used in capital cases and then had the subjects define mitigating and aggravating circumstances. Only 64 percent of the subjects were correct or partially correct for aggravating circumstances and only 47 percent for mitigating circumstances. Thus, the instructions do not appear to be clear to prospective jurors.

Wiener et al. (1995) gave people different forms of jury instructions after having them listen to a capital case. They found that baseline instructions were the least understood, while a version of the instructions that they devised were the best understood. Those who were least confused by the instructions were less likely to impose the death penalty.

Discussion

On the whole, the knowledge that a guilty verdict may result in a death sentence appears to have an impact on jurors. The research also raises the issue of whether the same jury should assess guilt and assign a sentence.

The majority of the studies indicated that potential jurors who are death-qualified on either the *Witherspoon* or the *Witt* criteria are likely to render different verdicts and assign different sentences than potential jurors who are not death-qualified and who are excludable. The implication of this finding to some scholars is that it provides an argument against the death penalty. However, one of the principles of the

American criminal justice system is to *avoid* having a random selection
of the general public as jurors. Potential jurors may be eliminated for
a variety of reasons, and both defense and prosecution lawyers are
permitted to challenge jurors. In addition, lawyers for both the
defense and prosecution sometimes employ consultants to advise
them on jury selection so that they may arrive at a jury favorable to
their position. As long as challenges to jurors and jury consultants are
allowed in jury trials in general, there would appear to be no good
rationale for not excluding some potential jurors in capital trials.

This issue is made more salient because the American criminal justice system, like those in many other countries, is based on the notion
that a just verdict is best arrived at by an untrained, non-professional
set of jurors rather than by establishing a profession of "jurors" who
are trained in the criminal justice system and who develop experience
in the course of their career in judging and sentencing for particular
crimes.

REFERENCES

Bernard, J., & Dwyer, W. Witherspoon v. Illinois. *Law and Psychology Review*, 1984,
    8, 105-114.
Cowan, C., Thompson, W., & Ellsworth, P. The effects of death qualification on
    jurors' predisposition to convict and on the quality of deliberation. *Law and
    Human Behavior*, 1984, 8, 53-79.
Cox, M., & Tanford, S. An alternative method of jury selection. *Law and Human
    Behavior*, 1989, 13, 167-183.
Elliott, R., & Robinson, R. J. Death penalty attitudes and the tendency to acquit or
    convict. *Law and Human Behavior*, 1991, 15, 389-404.
Ellsworth, P., Bukaty, R., Cowan, C., & Thompson, W. The death-qualified jury and
    the defense of insanity. *Law and Human Behavior*, 1984, 8, 81-93.
Ellsworth, P., & Ross, L. Public opinion and capital punishment. *Crime and
    Delinquency*, 1983, 29, 116-169.
Finkel, N. J., & Duff, K. B. Felony-murder and community sentiment. *Law and
    Human Behavior*, 1991, 15, 405-429.
Finkel, N. J., Hughes, K. C., Smith, S. F., & Hurabiell, M. L. Killing kids. *Behavioral
    Sciences and the Law*, 1994, 12(1), 5-20.
Finkel, N. J., & Smith, S. F. Principals and accessories in capital felony-murder. *Law
    and Society Review*, 1993, 27(1), 129-156.
Fitzgerald, R., & Ellsworth, P. Due process vs crime control. *Law and Human
    Behavior*, 1984, 8, 31-51.

Freedman, J. L. The effect of capital punishment on jurors' willingness to convict. *Journal of Applied Social Psychology*, 1990, 20, 465-477.

Gleason, J., & Harris, V. Group dimension and defendant's socioeconomic status as determinants of judgments by simulated jurors. *Journal of Applied Social Psychology*, 1976, 6, 186-191.

Hamilton, V., & Rotkin, L. The capital punishment debate. *Journal of Applied Social Psychology*, 1979, 9, 350-376.

Haney, C. On the selection of capital juries. *Law and Human Behavior*, 1984, 8, 121-132.

Haney, C., Hurtado, A., & Vega, L. "Modern" death qualification. *Law and Human Behavior*, 1994, 18, 619-633.

Haney, C., & Lynch, M. Comprehending life and death matters. *Law and Human Behavior*, 1994, 18, 411-436.

Hendrick, C., & Shaffer, D. Murder. *Bulletin of the Psychonomic Society*, 1975, 6, 313-316.

Hester, R., & Smith, R. Effects of a mandatory death penalty on the decisions of simulated jurors as a function of heinousness of the crime. *Journal of Criminal Justice*, 1973, 1, 319-326.

Horowitz, I. A., & Seguin, D. G. The effects of bifurcation and death qualification on assignment of penalty in capital crimes. *Journal of Applied Social Psychology*, 1986, 16, 165-185.

Jurow, G. New data on the effect of a "death qualified" jury on the guilt determination process. *Harvard Law Review*, 1971, 84, 567-611.

Luginbuhl, J. Comprehension of judges' instructions in the penalty phase of a capital trial. *Law and Human Behavior*, 1992, 16, 203-218.

Luginbuhl, J., & Middendorf, K. Death penalty beliefs and jurors' responses to aggravating and mitigating circumstances in capital trials. *Law and Human Behavior*, 1988, 12, 263-281.

McShane, M. D., Williams, F. P., & Pelfrey, W. V. Eligibility for jury service in capital trials. *Texas Bar Journal*, 1987, 50, 365-370.

Moran, G., & Comfort, J. C. Neither "tentative" nor "fragmentary." *Journal of Applied Psychology*, 1986, 71, 146-155.

Nieses, M. L., & Dillehay, R. C. Death qualification and conviction proneness. *Behavioral Sciences and the Law*, 1987, 5, 479-494.

Nietzel, M. T., Dillehay, R. C., & Himelein, M. J. Effects of Voir Dire variations in capital trials. *Behavioral Sciences and the Law*, 1987, 5, 467-477.

Robinson, R. J. What does "unwilling" to impose the death penalty mean anyway? *Law and Human Behavior*, 1993, 17, 471-477.

Seltzer, R., Lopes, G., Dayan, M., & Canan, R. The effect of death qualification on the propensity of jurors to convict. *Howard Law Journal*, 1987, 29, 571-607.

Seltzer, R., & McCormick, J. P. The impact of crime victimization and fear of crime on attitudes toward death penalty defendants. *Violence and Victims*, 1987, 2, 99-114.

Thompson, W., Cowan, C., & Ellsworth, P. Death penalty attitudes and conviction proneness. *Law and Human Behavior*, 1984, 8, 95-113.

White, L. T. Juror decision making in the capital penalty trial. *Law and Human Behavior*, 1987, 11, 113-130.

Wiener, R. L., Pritchard, C. C., & Weston, M. Comprehensibility of approved jury instructions in capital murder cases. *Journal of Applied Psychology*, 1995, 80, 455-467.

Williams, F. P., & McShane, M. D. Inclinations of prospective jurors in capital cases. *Sociology and Social Research*, 1990, 74, 85-94.

Chapter 9

ECONOMIC ANALYSIS OF THE DETERRENT EFFECT OF THE DEATH PENALTY

BIJOU YANG[1]

People often have ambivalent attitudes toward the death penalty. Murderers ought to be punished for their crimes. Yet, is ending another human's life an appropriate method of punishment?

What is the purpose of capital punishment? If the death penalty cannot deter the crime of murder, would the public approve of such a punishment? The possible deterrent effect of capital punishment has been a controversial issue for many years. To understand the controversy, first we have to learn about the rationale behind capital punishment. There are three theories as to why executions might result in a decrease in homicide: deterrence, normative validation, and victim mobilization (Gibbs, 1975). The deterrent view argues that the homicide rate will drop due to a fear of punishment. Normative validation, in contrast, contends that an execution reduces the homicide rate by validating the norm that it is wrong to kill. Finally, victim mobilization posits that the homicide rate drops after an execution due to potential victims taking extra precautions against violence (Stack, 1995).

On the other hand, some argue that capital punishment may stimulate more murder, a brutalization effect. There are three explanations as to why capital punishment may increase the murder rate (Stack, 1993). The first is that executions increase the homicide rate by promoting "lethal vengeance" or "execution identification." Executions demonstrate that it is appropriate to kill those who have gravely offended us.

A second possibility is identification with the victim in the execution–"victim identification." In this, the homicide rate increases after

---

1. Associate Professor of Economics, Drexel University.

an execution due to the presence of a group of suicidal/homicidal persons in the population. Such persons have a deep-seated hatred of themselves and others and murder in order to commit suicide by execution.

Increases in the homicide rate after an execution can also be triggered by imitation of the crimes of the condemned. Troubled persons may become fascinated with such crimes to the point of copying the behavior (Bowers & Pierce, 1980).

When the deterrent effect of capital punishment is not significantly supported by the data, proponents of capital punishment usually are not persuaded by the findings. Some have argued that, during periods when executions are few in number, capital punishment is less effective as a deterrent to murder (van den Haag, 1969, 1975, 1978; van den Haag & Conrad, 1983; Lehtinen, 1977). It is possible that a certain level of execution certainty (a threshold point) must be achieved before executions and execution publicity become effective deterrents to murder (Bailey, 1990).

At times, the findings of non-significance of the deterrence of capital punishment might reflect the social context surrounding capital punishment, such as during the 1960s and early 1970s. Those were the years when there was a great deal of skepticism and ambivalence regarding the role and utility of the death penalty in this country. This ambivalence was reflected in a decline in the use of capital punishment and a questioning of its constitutional legitimacy as a criminal sanction (Bailey & Peterson, 1987).

This chapter reviews the research on the deterrent effect of the death penalty from an econometric perspective since so much of research has been conducted by economists and has appeared in economic journals. The first section briefly reviews the methodological issues in the research. The second section will discuss a general economic model of murder. Next, the controversy surrounding Ehrlich's research on the topic, and time-series studies on the United States and on individual states will be discussed. The deterrent effect of media publicity for executions will be examined. Finally, some conclusions will be drawn in the last section.

A Review of Methodological Issues

Theories about the deterrent effect of the death penalty are at least two centuries old. In the eighteenth century, Cesare Beccaria was one of the first scholars to argue against capital punishment in his book, *Dei Delettie Dele Pene.* He argued that it was better to prevent crimes than to punish them. Jeremy Bentham argued later in the same century in *The Rationale of Punishment* that punishment should be designed to discourage greater "evil," under the supposition that each person behaves according to "felicific calculus" (Klein et al., 1978).

Scanty data and limited computational capabilities prevented empirical studies of the deterrent effect of the death penalty until the 1950s. The period of the 1950s and 1960s was characterized primarily by the comparative methodology made popular by Thorsten Sellin (Peterson & Bailey, 1988). During this period, the most common approach to testing the deterrent effect of the death penalty was to compare homicide rates in jurisdictions with the death penalty (retentionist states) and those without (abolitionist states) (Bye, 1919; Savitz, 1958; Schuessler, 1952; Sellin, 1967; Sutherland, 1925). The deterrence hypothesis is that murder rates should be higher in abolitionist than in death penalty states. An alternative source of evidence came from comparative analysis of homicide rates from states before and after the abolition and/or reinstatement of the death penalty (Bedau, 1967; Schuessler, 1952; Sellin, 1955, 1959, 1967). Here the deterrence hypothesis predicts that abolition of the death penalty should be followed by an increase in the murder rate, and conversely, reinstatement should result in a decrease in the murder rate.

Sellin compared groups of contiguous states, abolitionist versus retentionist. These states were examined for their similarity on a variety of socioeconomic and demographic characteristics. Sellin discovered that the homicide rates of retentionist states did not generally differ over time from the homicide rates of abolitionist states. From this study, he drew "the inevitable conclusion" that executions have no discernible effect on homicide rates.

The current interest of economists in criminal behavior began with Becker's (1968) theoretical analysis of both the individual's criminal behavior and society's response to crime. This model of individual criminal behavior was extended and subjected to elaborated empirical tests by Ehrlich (1973, 1975). Ehrlich's empirical tests supported an economic model of criminal behavior, one part of which was that capital punishment has a deterrent effect because individuals, including criminals, respond to the incentives and penalties embodied in the justice system.

Ehrlich's most famous finding was that one execution per year over the period that he studied (1933 to 1969) would have resulted in seven or eight fewer murders. Ehrlich's conclusion provoked a storm of controversy, which intensified because, in a constitutional challenge to the death penalty then pending in the United States Supreme Court (*Fowler v. North Carolina*), the solicitor general presented Ehrlich's findings to the Court, and in his amicus brief cited them as important empirical support that the death penalty deters murderers (Baldus & Cole, 1975).

Ehrlich (1973), following Becker (1968), developed models which address the economic motivations and choices for individuals who engage in some combination of legitimate and illegitimate activities to maximize their utility. According to Cloninger (1992), these choices may be viewed as the selection of a portfolio consisting of some combination of riskless (legitimate) assets and risky (criminal) assets with each asset bearing its respective expected return. The specific portfolio chosen would depend upon the individual's degree of risk aversion and the expected return received per unit of risk incurred.

This analysis parallels, in part, the development of portfolio theory by Markowitz (1959) with subsequent elaborations by Sharpe (1963, 1964), Lintner (1965) and Nossin (1966) with regard to asset portfolios. Markowitz showed that the risk from holding assets could be reduced by holding more than one asset at a time as long as the assets' returns are less than perfectly positively correlated. Sharpe demonstrated that the returns of individual assets can be related to a total market index of returns rather than the returns of every individual asset. The risk of a specific asset can then be measured by its beta–the degree to which its returns are correlated with those of the market portfolio–because all other variations can be diversified away by holding a portfolio of assets.

The empirical evidence found in the Cloninger's study in applying the portfolio approach to murders supported the economic model developed by Becker and the empirical results of Ehrlich, among others.

Yang and Lester (1994) suggest two possible flaws in Cloninger's analysis: (1) The beta used in Cloninger's study to measure the risk of criminal offenses may be misleading because it did not reflect the severity of the crime. The weighting scheme developed by Sellin and Wolfgang (1971) could be used to assign each crime a weight to reflect its impact on society. (2) Cloninger did not examine the impact of more than one execution in a given year. Lester (1987) has found that the impact of one or more executions in year n in a given state on the number of homicides in the state varies with the number of executions.

Another interesting issue involved in the discussion of death penalty in the economic literature is the welfare economics of capital punishment. There is a large related literature on the welfare economics of punishment (Becker, 1968; Harris, 1970; Stigler, 1970; Stern, 1978; Lee, 1983; Bone, 1985; McDonald, 1987) which is virtually silent on the issue of capital punishment (Cameron, 1989). Sesnowitz and McKee (1977, p. 217) were the first to argue that justifying capital punishment on deterrence grounds "does not survive the logical application of economic welfare criteria," because a world with capital punishment must have a lower welfare level than one without it, regardless of the actual magnitude of any deterrence effects. This is based on the consideration that there is no sufficient sum of money which can be used to compensate for the life of an executed individual.

However, other researchers have offered a counter-argument by pointing out that criminal's welfare should not be included in the social welfare function (Reynolds, 1977). According to Cameron (1989), a different approach to deriving propositions about which individuals' benefits should be included in the welfare function comes from contractarianism. Under a contractarian model, the murderer forfeits the right not to be murdered because of breaking an earlier accord in which murdering rights were traded for something else such as protection from being murdered.

Murder generates externality to the society. An externality is the impact of an action which affects a third party. In the case of murders, the impact felt by people other than murderers and victims are counted as part of externalities. Capital punishment is considered to be an abatement technology for externalities. It may however generate further externalities from its operation. These include the brutalization effect, "perverse deterrence," and the costs to the society of executing innocent defendants (Cameron, 1989). The brutalization hypothesis argues that the taking of life by the government lowers respect for life and fosters a more violent social climate, with this being a positive function of the visibility of the execution. The perverse deterrence argument is that some individuals will randomly murder in order to receive the death penalty. The perverse deterrence and brutalization arguments suggest that capital punishment may lead to more murders and/or more other crimes. Evidence for brutalization is provided in Espy (1980), Phillips (1980) and Bowers and Pierce (1984), and evidence for perverse deterrence in Espy (1980) and Glaser (1977).

Other issues investigated in the literature include measurement error, simultaneous equation bias, the identification problem, the influence of prior beliefs, the issue of non-stationarity, and some more advanced econometric techniques.

One common error (typically viewed as a measurement error by economists) occurring in empirical analyses concerns the construction of variables used as proxies for the risk of punishment and the severity of punishment (Avio, 1988). A standard example (Cook, 1977; Pyle, 1983) involves regressing the risk of capture (and other variables) upon the crime rate. The recorded number of offenses is used as both the numerator for the crime rate (offenses per unit of the population) and as the denominator for the risk of capture (clearances per offense). Avio (1988) investigated this particular measurement error and reported that in every case the estimated coefficients for the conditional risk of execution became "stronger" when it occurs in the data. This means that the deterrent effect may be exaggerated.

Since the death penalty is the result of the interplay of criminal behavior and the behavior of the criminal justice system, it makes sense to establish a system of equations which captures not only criminal behavior but also the behavior of the justice system. Chressanthis (1989) tested the relationship between criminal homicide rates in the United States for the period 1965 to 1985 and the deterrent effect of capital punishment by utilizing a recursive system method. The analysis revealed that not only did a deterrent effect of capital punishment exist but also that changes in commonly selected law enforcement, judicial, demographic, and economic control variables were significant in a manner consistent with implications from general theoretical models of criminal behavior.

Hoenack et al. (1978) and Hoenack and Weiler (1980) demonstrated that Ehrlich's faulty analysis results from a failure to recognize the importance of the identification problem. The identification problem exists when observed data representing specific values of variables are causally generated by more than one behavioral relationship among the variables. The problem involves attributing to particular behavioral relationships their unique influences in the causal generation of the data. In both studies by Hoenack, a structural model was established which represented the behavior of murderers, the criminal justice system, and the society in causally generating observations. For the years 1933 to 1969, the estimated results from Hoenack's model suggested that Ehrlich's estimated equation could have been causally generated by the response of the criminal justice system to murder, rather than as a result of the deterrent effect. In other words, within a given time period and with fixed resources available to the criminal justice system, an increase in capital murders will lead to decreases in apprehensions, convictions, and executions.[2] The seemingly negative association between the murders and those risk variables thus emerges because of the way the system works, rather than as a result of the deterrent effect.

As the validity of the deterrence effect is pivotal in providing support for the death penalty, it is not surprising to find the debate on the subject so controversial and passionate. The nature of the debate undermines the research in such a manner that investigators usually approach the issue of the deterrent effect of capital punishment with biased prior beliefs. Some believe that punishments deter and that social and economic variables have little or no influence on the murder rate. Others believe that punishments have little or no impact and that variations in the murder rate between states (or over time) can be explained by variations in economic and social conditions. McManus (1985) utilized a Bayesian econometric technique, proposed by Leamer (1978), to explore the impact of several possible alternative prior beliefs by researchers concerning the determinants of the murder rate using cross-national data from 1950. The deterrent effect was not sufficiently strong so as to lead researchers with different prior beliefs to reach a consensus regarding the deterrent effect of capital punishment.

---

2. Hoenack appears to have a misprint in his report concerning this.

On the issue of non-stationarity, Cover and Thistle (1988) showed that the United States homicide rate is a non-stationary time series. It is well known that the use of non-stationary series in regression analyses leads to inconsistent coefficient estimators, biased estimators of coefficient standard errors toward zero, and invalidates standard statistical-inference procedures (Davison et al., 1985; Granger & Newbold, 1974; Nelson & Kang, 1981; 1983; Nelson & Plosser, 1982; Plosser et al., 1982; Plosser & Schwert, 1978). Non-stationarity may be due to a linear trend (the so-called trend non-stationarity) or may be a property of the underlying stochastic process (the so-called difference non-stationarity).

Cover and Thistle suggested that a non-stationary series such as the United States homicide rate must be differenced in order to achieve stationarity. A linear time trend does not correct for the non-stationarity of the homicide rate. As is now well known, the use of non-stationary time series and the inappropriate use of a time trend lead to spurious regressions. Once the data were differenced, Cover and Thistle found that the results of tests of the deterrence hypothesis were sensitive to the empirical definitions of the probabilities of arrest, conviction, and execution. These empirical results implied that the United States time-series data did not provide unambiguous support for the deterrence hypothesis.

Finally, more advanced econometric techniques employed in examining the deterrent effect include extreme bound analysis (developed by Leamer [1978, 1983] and Leamer and Leonard [1983]) and bootstrapping (developed by Efron [1979]). While the former refers to an inference based on the range of point estimates of the coefficient of concern, the latter refers to a simulation procedure to set up artificial samples in order to estimate the coefficients of concern. McAleer et al. (1985) noted that the extreme bounds are usually generated by the imposition of highly arbitrary and unknown restrictions between the parameters of a model. Instead, they proposed a three-stage approach to modeling, involving the selection and subsequent simplification of a general model and a rigorous evaluation of the preferred model. McAleer and Veall (1989) applied the bootstrap method to the deterrent effect and showed that the bootstrap estimates of the extreme bounds are sometimes so large as to cast doubts on the usefulness of the bounds. Veall (1992) later used the data employed in Leamer (1983) and McManus (1985) and concluded that the bootstrap approach appears to give reasonable results, although the results differ according to the choice of regression strategy.

An Economic Model of Murder

The model presented here is based primarily on the work of Palmer (1977), which provides a basic framework for how criminal behavior is treated in economics. Committing a crime is treated by economists as an act of rational behavior by criminals. An individual is acting "rationally" if, given a choice between various alternatives, he selects what seems to be the most desirable or the least undesirable alternative.

In economic theory, the decision to commit a murder depends upon the benefits and costs associated with murder and with alternative legitimate activities. An individual will commit fewer murders if the benefits from crime decrease, the costs of crime increase or the costs of legitimate activities decrease.

The benefits from crime consist of the pecuniary return (the money and goods obtained from the crime) and non-pecuniary returns such as the enjoyment which comes directly from the crime itself.

Economic theory identifies several costs incurred in criminal activity. They included (1) the money spent on obtaining the equipment and information needed to commit the murder, (2) the psychic cost or the displeasure caused by the murder, (3) the opportunity costs, that is, the net gain from the time spent in legitimate activities, and (4) the expected loss due to punishment for the crime which is an average of possible punishments, weighted by the probability of conviction and punishment.

An individual will engage in murder only if its benefits are greater than all of the costs mentioned above. Therefore, economic theory suggests that the number of murders can be reduced by increasing its costs or by decreasing its benefits. The latter involves methods for reducing the pecuniary and non-pecuniary returns from murder, while the former consists of methods for increasing the cost of resources needed to commit the crime, the opportunity cost and the cost of punishment.

When considering the problem of reducing the number of murders, economists are more concerned than are other social scientists with the methods that will increase the opportunity costs, such as raising the wage rate for legitimate activities and reducing the unemployment rates. To a lesser degree, economists are also concerned with increasing the cost of punishment by increasing probability of conviction and increasing the severity of punishment. Having a death penalty also increases the cost of committing a crime since the murder will no longer be able to engage in productive legitimate activities in the future.

As long as we assume that criminals react to punishments and incentives as Ehrlich emphasized in his writing, the death penalty will work to increase the cost of criminal activities, other things being equal, and the potential criminal will be less motivated to commit murders.

In measuring the deterrent effect of the death penalty, Ehrlich was the first to employ a regression analysis. The regression analysis has the advantage of embracing simultaneously all the independent variables that affect the behavior of murder. It therefore examines the deterrent effect in the context of a broader model of criminal behavior than does more traditional comparative methodology. For example, to explain the crime rate, Ehrlich (1975) used the probability of arrest, the conditional probability of conviction, the conditional probability of execution, the labor participation rate, the unemployment rate, the proportion of the population aged 14 to 24, the permanent income per capita, the proportion of non-whites in the population, the per capita expenditures of all government agencies, the per capita expenditures on police, and the time variable.

The data used in the regression analysis of the deterrent effect of the death penalty by various investigators have included national and state data and have been time-series and cross-sectional. Ehrlich used national data for the United States compiled by the FBI for the period of 1933 to 1969. He employed a log-linear form of the model to estimate the deterrent effect of the death penalty and found that the elasticity of the execution rate was negatively related to the murder rate. The order of magnitude of the effect suggested that one execution might prevent seven or eight murders a year during the period he studied.

Another economic model to test the deterrence hypothesis has been developed by Yunker (1976). Yunker employed a cobweb model of homicide rate-execution interaction to test the deterrent effect of the death penalty. In his model, there are two basic postulates, namely, (1) current executions are positively related to the current homicide rate, and (2) the current homicide rate is inversely related to the past level of executions. In other words, Yunker hypothesized that, if the current homicide rate is high, the current execution rate would also be high, yet the high execution rate will reduce the homicide rate in the near future.

Yunker also carried out a time-series regression analysis on the United States from 1933 to 1959 and 1960 to 1972. For the first time period, the execution rate was positively related to the murder rate, while for the second period the association was negative (supporting a deterrent effect). For the period 1933 to 1972 as a whole, the association was not significantly differently from zero.

Yunker's approach and conclusions were completely rejected by Fox (1977) because of statistical issues concerning improper model identification, dubious "data-mining" procedures, "flimsy" results that failed to account for simultaneity of the modeled relationships, problems centered around recursive systems, and ad hoc model specification. Furthermore, Fox charged that Yunker allowed his bias in favor of capital punishment to slant his analysis.

Criticisms of Ehrlich's Work

Ehrlich's model and approach have been criticized extensively on a number of grounds (Layson, 1985). Among the criticisms of Ehrlich's time-series work on homicide, the most important are: (1) The FBI data used by Ehrlich to measure homicide and the probabilities of punishment are highly suspect, especially during the 1930s. (2) Ehrlich's results are sensitive to the inclusion of additional explanatory variables and the choice of functional form. (3) Ehrlich's regressions are unstable over the 1960s. (4) The negative correlation between the homicide rate and the probabilities of punishment found by Ehrlich may be explained by the effect of the homicide rate on the probabilities of punishment rather than vice versa.

For example, both Passell and Taylor (1977) and Bowers and Pierce (1975) attempted to replicate Ehrlich's results and discovered that the strength of the deterrent effect of the death penalty was dependent upon the choice of a logarithmic form for the model under estimation. These investigators also found that the deterrent effect was not significant when data from the 1960s were excluded from the regression analysis. During this period, there was a sudden rapid increase of crime of all types, including murder, while both the average length of prison terms and the probability of execution declined.

Baldus and Cole (1975) suggested that Ehrlich's use of national data obscured the relationship between murder and execution rates and may have yielded results which seem consistent with a deterrent effect when no such effect actually exists. They also pointed out that Ehrlich's analysis focused on the marginal effects of small changes in the execution risk rather than on the difference between jurisdictions which do or do not use capital punishment.

Beyleveld (1982) criticized Ehrlich's methodology and came to the following conclusions. (1) Ehrlich saw his key assumption of utility theory as an "heuristic" integrating assumption with general application, whereas it should be viewed as specifying a possible mechanism to define and explain only one possible category of human behavior, since it is not true by definition that all human behavior is a process of utility maximization. (2) Ehrlich's strategy, particularly in drawing policy implications, relied upon a predictive criterion for the adequacy of a theory which cannot do the work demanded of it.

There have been numerous other statistical analyses testing the deterrent effect of the death penalty. Four types of research can be identified: (1) time-series studies on the United States as a whole, (2) time-series studies on individual states, (3) cross-sectional studies, and (4) the impact of execution publicity. Each category will be reviewed in separate sections.

Time-Series Studies on the United States as a Whole

Ehrlich's research focused on the period 1933 to 1969. Other periods have been chosen for study by other investigators, for example, Bechdolt (1977) who studied 1949 to 1974 and Kleck (1979) who studied 1947 to 1973. Bechdolt found a significant deterrent effect from executions on both the murder and the rape rates, but when he split the period into two subperiods (1949 to 1962 and 1963 to 1974) he found no significant deterrent effect for either subperiod. Kleck found no deterrent effect from the execution rate on the murder rate.

Shin (1978) chose the period 1930 to 1971 and carried out two separate time-series analyses using different sets of explanatory variables. The results were opposite in the two analyses. In the first he found a significant positive association between the execution rate and the murder rate (that is, a brutalization effect), while in the second he found a non-significant association.

Sesnowitz and McKee (1977) selected a longer period for study, 1906 to 1972. They repeated Yunker's analysis and found a negative association between the number of executions and the murder rate. They noted, however, that executions were also negatively related to the rate of theft, and so they argued that a negative association between execution and murder did not prove a deterrent effect.

Layson (1985) updated estimates of the United States homicide function for the period of 1936 to 1977 that strongly confirmed Ehrlich's deterrence findings. In that study the homicide rate was measured using the Vital Statistics measure of homicide rather than the FBI series. He found that the Vital Statistics data supported the deterrence theory more strongly than the FBI series.

Time-Series Analyses on Individual States

Single-state analyses have been conducted in California, Ohio, New York, and Illinois, with varied results. For California, Bailey (1979a) studied 1920 to 1962 and found no significant association between the execution rate and the murder rate, both with and without a time lag. For Ohio, Bailey (1979b) also found no significant association, with and without a logarithmic transformation of the data. For New York State, Bowers and Pierce (1980) looked at monthly data for the period 1907 to 1963. They found a significant increase in murders in the month after an execution (and only in that month), but only when they controlled for the time trend in the rates using fourth order and higher polynomials (and not for lower order polynomials).

For Illinois, Decker and Kohfeld (1984) studied the period 1933 to 1980 and found a non-significant negative association between the execution rate and the murder rate. With a one-year time lag, the negative correlation was significant, supporting a deterrent effect. When they carried out a multiple regression, using socio-demographic variables, the effect of executions was no longer significant. They focused on this latter finding and concluded that there was no deterrent effect from executions.

A multi-state study was carried out by Bailey (1979-1980). He included 37 states for which data were available. For twenty-four states, the regression coefficient was negative (indicating a deterrent effect); for eight states, the regression coefficient was positive (indicating a brutality effect); and for five other states it was zero. In the multiple regression for some states, executions ranked as the second most important variable. (There was no relationship between the size of the regression coefficient and the average murder rate of the states.) Analyses using a one-year time lag did not support deterrent effect.

A single-city study was conducted by Bailey (1983a). For Chicago from 1915 to 1921, the number of executions was positively related to the number of homicides each month, but not significantly so. A multiple regression using control variables produced a similar result.

Grogger (1990) employed an analysis of daily time-series of homicides in California to test for the short-term deterrent effect of capital punishment. For each category of homicide examined, the procedure did not detect a deterrent effect during a two-week to four-week period immediately surrounding the executions.

Cross-Sectional Studies

The two years 1950 and 1960 have been most often chosen for cross-sectional analyses. The majority of studies have reported either a non-significant correlation between execution rates and homicide rates or a positive one. For example, Passell (1975) studied forty-one states in 1950 and forty-four states in 1960 and found no significant associations. (Controls for whether the states had a death penalty and whether those with a death penalty executed anyone did not change the failure to find a deterrent effect.) However, Passell found that the simple correlation between murder rates and the execution rate was positive.

Bailey (1977) looked at the effect of the execution rate on the first-degree murder rate in 1950 and 1960. For both years, the correlation was not significantly different from zero, either in the simple correlation or in a multiple regression. (Data from 1920, 1930, and 1940 gave similar results.)

Boyes and McPheters (1977) carried out an analysis for forty-seven states in 1960 and found no association between the execution rate and the rape rate.

Black and Orsagh (1978) looked at all states in 1950 and 1960. Using multiple regressions with unweighted and weighted variables (weighted, for example, by the state's population), they found either non-significant or positive associations.

Bailey (1980b) examined the forty states that executed criminals in 1960 and found that the rate of executions and the time between sentencing and execution were both unrelated to the homicide rate. When Bailey used a logarithmic transformation of the data, he found a negative association with the celerity of the executions (the opposite of a deterrent effect) and a positive association with the rate of executions (also the opposite of a deterrent effect).

Bailey (1983b) later looked at *changes* in the execution rates and the homicide rates from 1950 to 1960 for states with a death penalty. The change in the execution rate was not related to the change in the homicide rate. Forst (1977) also looked at changes in the execution rate and the homicide rate from 1960 to 1970 for thirty-two states, and he too found no significant effect from changes in the execution rate on the homicide rate using a multiple regression analysis. (Since there were no executions in 1970, it would have made sense to choose two years when there were executions.)

In contrast to the results of these studies, Cloninger (1977) reported that the execution rate in 1960 was negatively associated with the murder rate, indicating a deterrent effect. This association was found for the thirty-two non-Southern states, but not for the sixteen Southern states.

Studies of years other than 1950 and 1960 have also produced inconclusive results. Bailey (1974) examined data for 1967 and 1968 for first- and second-degree murder. For twenty-seven states in the sample with a death penalty, the correlations between the execution rate and the murder rate were all negative (indicating a deterrent effect) and reached statistical significance for the total murder rate in 1968. Bailey (1975) correlated the execution rates for the period 1962 to 1966 with the murder rate in 1967 and 1968. The correlations were all negative, supporting a deterrent effect, and two were statistically significant. Bailey (1976) studied sixteen states with a death penalty for rape in 1951 and 1961 and found a deterrent effect for both years.

Ehrlich (1977) conducted a cross-sectional analysis over the states for 1940 and 1950 and reported that the execution rate was significantly related to the homicide rate in the direction of a deterrent effect, even when other variables were included in the analysis.

Bailey (1980a) later correlated the execution rate and socio-demographic variables with the homicide rate over at least thirty-nine of the states for each year in the period 1920 to 1962. Twenty of the simple correlations between the execution rate and the homicide rate were negative, seven were positive and one was zero. With a one-year time lag, only sixteen were negative as compared to twelve positive. This study seems to support a deterrent effect.

Other cross-sectional studies have found a brutalization effect. Bechdolt (1977) carried out a cross-sectional study using 1970 homicide rates and the number of executions in each state during the 1960s. He found a positive association between executions and homicide rates, suggesting a brutalization effect. (By 1970, executions were no longer taking place in the United States, and so there was no effective death penalty.) Glaser (1977) showed that the more executions in a retentionist state from 1930 to 1970, the higher the homicide rates during 1960 to 1975, the less time served by murderers before parole and the less time served by murderers before their first release. (However, the abolitionist states did not fit into this linear trend, behaving more like the retentionist states with a moderate number of executions.)

A unique longitudinal study was carried out by Bailey and Lott (1977) comparing states before and after changing from a mandatory to a discretionary death penalty. They found that the form of the death penalty was unrelated to the homicide rate. Furthermore, execution rates did not change significantly after the switch. They also conducted cross-sectional studies and came to a similar conclusion.

Peterson and Bailey (1988) investigated the impact of the death penalty on state homicide rates for the post-*Furman* period, 1973 to 1984 (*Furman v. Georgia* was the case decided in 1972 by the United States Supreme Court that the death penalty as administered then was in violation of the Eighth and Fourteenth Amendments to the Constitution). The analysis found no indication that the national return to capital punishment since *Furman* led to a systematic downturn in the homicide rate.

Bailey and Peterson (1987) examined whether the death penalty provided protection to state policemen from fatal assaults for the post-*Furman* period. The data did not lend support to the deterrence hypothesis for these police officers murdered. Law enforcement officers were not afforded an added measure of protection by the death penalty in retentionist states as compared to abolitionist states, nor was there any significant association between the rate of police officers murdered and the frequency of the death sentence for convicted murderers in retentionist states.

The Impact of Execution Publicity

Fourteen studies dating from 1935 to 1993 have studied the impact of publicized executions. Seven have reported that publicized executions had no effect on the homicide rate (Bailey, 1990; Bailey & Peterson, 1989; Dann, 1935; King, 1978; McFarland, 1983; Savitz, 1958; Stack & Allen, 1991), two reported an increase in the homicide rate after a publicized execution (Bowers, 1989; Stack, 1993), four reported a decrease in the homicide rate (Phillips & Hensley, 1984; Stack, 1987, 1990; Stack & Gundlach, 1991), and one reported a decrease followed by an increase in the homicide rate (Phillips, 1980).

Recently, Stack (1995) applied Blumer's (1969) concept of differentiable audience receptivity to racial differences in reactions to publicized executions. He argued that African Americans are less responsive to punishment and labeling because they are already outsiders in a mostly Caucasian society and because they have a lower stake in conformity than do Caucasians. In accordance with his predictions, Stack found that publicized executions deterred Caucasian homicide rates but not African American homicide rates.

Bailey and Peterson (1989) reviewed an earlier investigation on the impact of execution publicity by Stack (1987) and found that it had a number of serious limitations, including technical coding errors, an unusual measure for the dependent variable, and omission of important deterrence, socio-demographic, and other factors associated with homicide rates. In addition, Stack ignored the possibility that the effect of executions may extend beyond execution months. Bailey and Peterson replicated and extended the Stack investigation, correcting for shortcomings in his analysis. Their results diverged substantially from Stack's. Once the technical coding errors were corrected, they were unable to find the significant inverse relationship between the levels of execution publicity and homicide rates.

Bailey (1990) also examined the monthly homicide rate and television publicity devoted to executions from 1976 through 1987. He found no evidence that the amount and/or type of television publicity devoted to execution had a significant deterrent or brutalization effect on homicide during the period.

Conclusion

Ever since Ehrlich published his work on the deterrent effect of the death penalty, which was based on economic theory and sophisticated econometric analyses, researchers have attempted similar analyses to support or refute his conclusions. The research has intensified and become more in-depth over the years. Overall, in time-series analyses and cross-sectional analyses on national data and individual states, the results have not been such that we can draw a clear conclusion about the deterrent effect of the death penalty.

Thus, the debate over the deterrence hypothesis is inconclusive. This debate has a long history and involves scholars from several disciplines, each of which has its own methodology, perspective and assumptions about human behavior. Because of these differences, it is not surprising that identical data sets can lead to different and contrary conclusions. At the present time, it is still fair to say, therefore, the debate continues.

REFERENCES

Avio, K. L. Measurement errors and capital punishment. *Applied Economics*, 1988, 20, 1253-1262.

Bailey, W. C. Murder and the death penalty. *Journal of Criminal Law and Criminology*, 1974, 65, 416-423.

Bailey, W. C. Murder and capital punishment. *American Journal of Orthopsychiatry*, 1975, 45, 669-688.

Bailey, W. C. Rape and the death penalty. In H. Bedau and C. Pierce (Eds.), *Capital punishment in the United States* (pp. 336-358). New York: AMS, 1976.

Bailey, W. C. Imprisonment versus the death penalty as a deterrent to murder. *Law and Human Behavior*, 1977, 1, 239-260.

Bailey, W. C. The deterrent effect of the death penalty for murder in California. *Southern California Law Review*, 1979a, 52, 743-764.

Bailey, W. C. The deterrent effect of the death penalty for murder in Ohio. *Cleveland State Law Review*, 1979b, 28, 51-70.

Bailey, W. C. Deterrent effect of the death penalty. *Omega*, 1979-1980, 10, 235-259.

Bailey, W. C. A multivariate cross-sectional analysis of the deterrent effect of the death penalty. *Sociology and Social Research*, 1980a, 64, 183-207.

Bailey, W. C. Deterrence and the celerity of the death penalty. *Social Forces,* 1980b, 58, 1308-1333.

Bailey, W. C. Disaggregation in deterrence and death penalty research. *Journal of Criminal Law and Criminology,* 1983a, 74, 827-859.

Bailey, W. C. The deterrent effect of capital punishment during the 1950s. *Suicide and Life-Threatening Behavior,* 1983b, 13, 95-107.

Bailey, W. C. Murder, capital punishment, and television: Execution publicity and homicide rates. *American Sociological Review,* 1990, 55, 628-633.

Bailey, W. C., & Lott, R. An empirical examination of the inutility of mandatory capital punishment. *Journal of Behavioral Economics,* 1977, 6, 153-188.

Bailey, W. C., & Peterson, R. D. Police killings and capital punishment: The post-*Furman* period. *Criminology,* 1987, 25, 1-25.

Bailey, W. C., & Peterson, R. Murder and capital punishment. *American Sociological Review,* 1989, 54, 722-743.

Baldus, D., & Cole, J. A comparison of the work of Thorsten Sellin and Isaac Ehrlich on the deterrent effect of capital punishment. *Yale Law Journal,* 1975, 18, 170-186.

Bechdolt, B. Capital punishment and homicide and rape rates in the United States. *Journal of Behavioral Economics,* 1977, 6, 33-66.

Becker, G. S. Crime and punishment: An economic approach. *Journal of Political Economy,* 1968, 76, 169-217

Bedau, H. *The death penalty in America.* (Rev. ed.) Garden City, NY: Doubleday, 1967.

Beyleveld, D. Ehrlich's analysis of deterrence. *British Journal of Criminology,* 1982, 22, 101-123.

Black, T., & Orsagh, T. New evidence of the efficacy of sanctions as a deterrent to homicide. *Social Science Quarterly,* 1978, 58, 616-631.

Blumer, H. Suggestions for the study of mass media effects. In H. Blumer (Ed.), *Symbolic interactionism* (pp. 183-194). Englewood Cliff, NJ: Prentice-Hall, 1969.

Bone, J. On substituting a socially costly penalty for costly crime. *International Review of Law and Economics,* 1985, 5, 239-246.

Bowers, W. J. The effects of executions is brutalization, not deterrence. In K. C. Haas & J. Inciardi (Eds.), *Adjudicating death* (pp. 49-89). Beverly Hills, CA: Sage, 1989.

Bowers, J., & Pierce, G. L. The illusion of deterrence in Isaac Ehrlich's research on capital punishment. *Yale Law Journal,* 1975, 85, 187-208.

Bowers, J., & Pierce, G. L. Deterrence or brutalization? *Crime and Delinquency,* 1980, 26, 493-484.

Bowers, J., & Pierce, G. L. *Legal homicide: Death as punishment in America 1864-1982.* Boston: Northeastern University Press, 1984.

Boyes, W., & McPheters, L. Capital punishment as a deterrent to violent crime. *Journal of Behavioral Economics,* 1977, 6, 67-86.

Bye, R. *Capital punishment in the United States.* Philadelphia: The committee on Philanthropic Labor of the Philadelphia Yearly Meeting of Friends, 1919.

Cameron, S. On the welfare economics of capital punishment. *Australian Economic Papers,* 1989, 28(53), 253-266.

Chressanthis, G. A. Capital punishment and the deterrent effect revisited: Recent time-series econometric evidence. *Journal of Behavioral Economics*, 1989, 18(2), 81-97.

Cloninger, D. O. Deterrence and the death penalty. *Journal of Behavioral Economics*, 1977, 6, 87-105.

Cloninger, D. O. Capital punishment and deterrence: A portfolio approach. *Applied Economics*, 1992, 24, 635-645.

Cook, P. J. Punishment and crime: A critique of current findings concerning the preventive effects of punishment. *Law and Contemporary Problems*, 1977, 41, 164-204.

Cover, J. P., & Thistle, P. D. Time series, homicide, and the deterrent effect of capital punishment. *Southern Economic Journal*, 1988, 54, 615-622.

Dann, R. H. The deterrent effect of capital punishment. *Friends' Social Service Series*, 1935, 29, 1-20.

Davison, R., Godfrey, L., & MacKinnon, J. G. A simplified version of the differencing test. *International Economic Review*, 1985, 26, 639-647.

Decker, S., & Kohfeld, C. A deterrence study of the death penalty in Illinois. *Journal of Criminal Justice*, 1984, 12, 367-377.

Efron, B. Bootstrap methods: Another look at the jackknife. *Annuals of Statistics*, 1979, 7, 1-26.

Ehrlich, I. The deterrent effect of capital punishment. *National Bureau of Economic Research. Working Paper Series*, No. 18, 1973.

Ehrlich, I. The deterrent effect of capital punishment: A question of life or death. *American Economic Review*, 1975, 65, 397-417.

Ehrlich, I. Capital punishment and deterrence. *Journal of Political Economy*, 1977, 85, 741-788.

Espy, M. W. Capital punishment and deterrence: What the statistics cannot show. *Crime and Delinquency*, 1980, 26, 537-544.

Fox, J. A. The identification and estimation of deterrence: An evaluation of Yunker's model. *Journal of Behavioral Economics*, 1977, 6(1/2), 225-242.

Forst, B. The deterrent effect of capital punishment. *Minnesota Law Review*, 1977, 61, 743-767.

Gibbs, J. *Crime, punishment, and deterrence.* New York: Elsevier, 1975.

Glaser, D. The realities of homicide versus the assumptions of economists in assessing capital punishment. *Journal of Behavioral Economics*, 1977, 6, 243-268.

Granger, C. W., & Newbold, P. Spurious regressions in econometrics. *Journal of Econometrics*, 1974, 2, 111-120.

Grogger, J. The deterrent effect of capital punishment: An analysis of daily homicide counts. *Journal of the American Statistical Association*, 1990, 85, 295-303.

Harris, J. R. On the economics of law and order. *Journal of Political Economy*, 1970, 78, 165-174.

Hoenack, S. A., Kudrle, R. T., & Sjoquist, D. L. The deterrent effect of capital punishment: A question of identification. *Policy Analysis*, 1978, 4, 491-527.

Hoenack, S. A., & Weiler, W. C. A structural model of murder behavior and the criminal justice system. *American Economic Review*, 1980, 70, 327-344.

King, D. R. The brutalization effect: Execution publicity and the incidence of homicide in South Carolina. *Social Forces*, 1978, 57, 683-687.

Kleck, G. Capital punishment, gun ownership and homicide. *American Journal of Sociology*, 1979, 84, 882-910.

Klein, L. R., Forst, B., & Filatov, V. The deterrent effect of capital punishment and assessment of the estimates. In A. Blumstein, J. Cohen and D. Nagin (Eds.), *Deterrence and incapacitation: Estimating the effects of criminal sanctions on crime rates* (pp. 336-360). Washington, DC: National Academy of Sciences, 1978.

Layson, S. K. Homicide and deterrence: A reexamination of the United States time-series evidence. *Southern Economic Journal*, 1985, 52(1), 68-89.

Leamer, E. E. *Specification searches: Ad hoc inference with nonexperimental data.* New York: Wiley, 1978.

Leamer, E. E. Let's take the con out of econometrics. *American Economic Review*, 1983, 73(1), 31-43.

Leamer, E. E., & Leonard, H. Reporting the fragility of regression estimates. *Review of Economics and Statistics*, 1983, 65, 306-317.

Lee, D. R. On substituting a socially costly penalty for costly crime. *International Review of Law and Economics*, 1983, 3, 179-185.

Lehtinen, M. W. The value of life: An argument for the death penalty. *Crime and Delinquency*, 1977, 23, 237-252.

Lester, D. *The death penalty.* Springfield, IL: Charles C Thomas, 1987.

Lintner, J. The valuation of risky assets and the selection of risky investments in stock portfolios and capital budgets. *Review of Economics and Statistics*, 1965, 47, 13-37.

Markowitz, H. M. *Portfolio selection: Efficient diversification of investment.* New York: Wiley, 1959.

McAleer, M., Pagan, A. R., & Volker, P. A. What will take the con out of econometrics? *American Economic Review*, 1985, 75(3), 293-307.

McAleer, M., & Veall, M. R. How fragile are fragile inferences? A re-evaluation of the deterrent effect of capital punishment. *Review of Economics and Statistics*, 1989, 71(1), 99-106.

McDonald, J. F. Crime and punishment: A social welfare analysis. *Journal of Criminal Justice*, 1987, 15, 245-254.

McFarland, S. Is capital punishment a short-term deterrent to homicide? *Journal of Criminal Law and Criminology*, 1983, 74, 1014-1030.

McManus, W. S. Estimates of the deterrent effect of capital punishment: The importance of the researcher's prior beliefs. *Journal of Political Economy*, 1985, 93, 417-425.

Nelson, C. R., & Kang, H. Spurious periodicity in inappropriately trended time series. *Econometrica*, 1981, 49, 741-751.

Nelson, C. R., & Kang, H. Pitfalls in the use of time as an explanatory variable in regression. *NBER Technical Working Papers*, No. 30, 1983.

Nelson, C. R., & Plosser, C. I. Trends and random walks in macroeconomic time series: Some evidence and implications. *Journal of Monetary Economics*, 1982, 10, 139-162.

Nossin, J. Equilibrium in a capital asset market. *Econometrica*, 1966, 34, 748-783.

Palmer, J. Economic analyses of the deterrent effect of capital punishment. *Journal of Research in Crime and Delinquency*, 1977, 14, 4-21.

Passell, P. The deterrent effect of death penalty. *Stanford Law Review*, 1975, 28, 61-80.

Passell, P., & Taylor, J. B. The deterrent effect of capital punishment: Another view. *American Economic Review*, 1977, 67, 445-451.

Peterson, R. D., & Bailey, W. C. Murder and capital punishment in the evolving context of the post-*Furman* era. *Social Forces*, 1988, 66, 774-807.

Phillips, D. P. The deterrence effect of capital punishment: New evidence on an old controversy. *American Journal of Sociology*, 1980, 86, 139-148.

Phillips, D. P., & Hensley, J. When violence is rewarded or punished: The impact of mass media stories on homicide. *Journal of Communication*, 1984, 34, 101-116.

Plosser, C. I., & Schwert, G. W. Money, income, and sunspots: Measuring economic relationships and the effects of differencing. *Journal of Monetary Economics*, 1978, 4, 637-660.

Plosser, C. I., Schwert, G. W., & White, H. Differencing as a test of specification. *International Economic Review*, 1982, 23, 535-552.

Pyle, D. J. *The economics of crime and law enforcement.* London: Macmillan, 1983.

Reynolds, M. O. On welfare economics of capital punishment. *American Journal of Economics and Sociology*, 1977, 36, 105-119.

Savitz, L. A study of capital punishment. *Journal of Criminal Law, Criminology, and Police Science*, 1958, 49, 338-341.

Schuessler, K. The deterrent effect of the death penalty. *Annals of the American Academy of Political and Social Science*, 1952, 284, 54-62.

Sellin, T. In *The Royal Commission on Capital Punishment (1949-1953)* (pp. 17-24). (Papers by Command 8932.) London, UK: H. M. Stationery Office, 1955.

Sellin, T. *The death penalty.* Philadelphia: American Law Institute, 1959.

Sellin, T. *Capital punishment.* New York: Harper & Row, 1967.

Sellin, T., & Wolfgang, M. E. Weighing crime. In L. Radzinowicz & M. E. Wolfgang (Eds.), *Crime and Justice, Volume 1: The Criminal in Society* (pp. 167-176). New York: Basic, 1971.

Sesnowitz, M., & McKee, D. On the deterrent effect of capital punishment. *Journal of Behavioral Economics*, 1977, 6, 217-224.

Sharpe, W. F. A simplified model for portfolio analysis. *Journal of Finance*, 1963, 9, 277-293.

Sharpe, W. F. Capital assets prices: A theory of market equilibrium under conditions of risk. *Journal of Finance*, 1964, 19, 425-442.

Shin, K. *Death penalty and crime.* Fairfax, VA: George Mason University, 1978.

Stack, S. Publicized executions and homicide, 1950-1980. *American Sociological Review*, 1987, 52, 532-540.

Stack, S. Execution publicity and homicide in South Carolina. *Sociological Quarterly*, 1990, 31, 599-611.

Stack, S. Execution publicity and homicide in Georgia. *American Journal of Criminal Justice*, 1993, 18, 25-39.

Stack, S. The impact of publicized executions on homicide. *Criminal Justice and Behavior*, 1995, 22, 172-186.

Stack, S., & Allen, W. The effect of executions on homicide in Alabama. Paper presented at the annual meeting of the Michigan Academy of Arts and Sciences, Ypsilanti, MI, April 1991.

Stack, S., & Gundlach, J. Still another look at execution publicity and homicide. Paper presented at the annual meeting of the American Sociological Association, Cincinnati, OH, August 1991.

Stern, N. On the economic theory of policy towards crime. In J. M. Heineke (Ed.), *Economic models of criminal behavior*. Amsterdam: North-Holland, 1978.

Stigler, G. J. The optimum enforcement of laws. *Journal of Political Economy*, 1970, 78, 526-536.

Sutherland, E. Murder and the death penalty. *Journal of the American Institute of Criminal Law and Criminology*, 1925, 51, 522-529.

van den Haag, E. On deterrence and the death penalty. *Journal of Criminal Law, Criminology and Police Science*, 1969, 60, 141-147.

van den Haag, E. In defense of the death penalty: A legal-practical-moral analysis. *Criminal Law Bulletin*, 1978, 14, 51-68.

van den Haag, E. *Punishing criminals*. New York: Basic Books, 1975.

van den Haag, E., & Conrad, J. *The death penalty*. New York: Plenum, 1983.

Veall, M. R. Bootstrapping the process of model selection: An econometric example. *Journal of Applied Econometrics*, 1992, 7, 93-99.

Yang, B., & Lester, D. Capital punishment and deterrence: A comment on Cloninger's paper. *Applied Economics Letters*, 1994, 1, 12-13.

Yunker, J. A. Is the death penalty a deterrent to homicide? Some time series evidence. *Journal of Behavioral Economics*, 1976, 5(1), 45-81.

Chapter 10

OTHER STUDIES OF DETERRENCE

Some research on the deterrent effect of the death penalty has been conducted using different methodologies from those used by economists. For example, some research has been conducted to see if executions have an impact during the immediate period after an execution. These and other studies on deterrence will be reviewed in this chapter.

Gary Gilmore's Execution

Lester (1980) found that Gary Gilmore's execution in 1977, the first for over a decade, had no significant effect on the national incidence of homicide in the following week or two-week period.

McFarland (1983) examined the effect on national homicide rates of the first four executions after 1976. He found that Gilmore's execution led to a significant decrease in the next two weeks, while the next three executions (Spenkelink, Bishop and Judy) had no effect. However, McFarland felt that the drop after Gilmore's execution was due to a spell of bad weather. He found the drop in the Midwestern states which experienced a blizzard, but not in the Western states where the weather remained fair.

It is worth noting that it is unlikely that one execution in a year in one state would have much of a national impact, and even unlikely that it would have much impact in the state of the execution. With 19,120 murders and non-negligent manslaughters in the USA in 1977, one execution does not represent a very high probability of execution.

Cochran et al. (1994) studied the impact of a single execution in Oklahoma on September 10, 1990, on the murder rate afterwards as compared to before. There were no significant changes in the total homicide rate or the felony murder rate, but there was an increase in the murder of strangers after the execution.

Changes from Year to Year

Lester (1973) studied the USA from 1955 to 1965. For 1962, states which executed someone were more likely to experience a drop in the number of homicides in 1963 than states without executions in 1962. Data from other years failed to reach significance. The deterrent effect was found for seven of the eleven years.

Building on this result, Lester (1979a, Appendix 3) studied the USA from 1930 to 1965. For the 828 occasions on which a state executed at least one person in a given year, the homicide incidence decreased in the following year in 53.6 percent of the instances. For the 818 occasions in which a state did not execute anyone, the homicide incidence decreased in 46.7 percent of the instances, a significant difference. This difference was found for years in which the incidence of homicide was increasing and for years in which it was decreasing.

Lester (1979b, Appendix 3) found that the likelihood of a decrease in the homicide incidence was greatest for 9–16 executions in a given year (69.2%), next greatest for 17–23 executions (61.1%), and least for 1–8 executions (51.8%). Looking at the proportion of executions (compared to murders), the likelihood of a decrease in the incidence of homicide rose from 51.7 percent for 0.0001–0.009 to 69.4 percent for 0.040–0.049, but then dropped to 43.6 percent for 0.050 or more.

Lester (Appendix 4) next calculated the correlation coefficients between measures of each state's execution practices in one year and the changes in the homicide rate from year to year. For four of the six possible combinations of measures, a weak deterrent effect was found.

Wasserman (1981) looked at states with a high rate of executions from 1930 to 1965 and found that they were more likely to have decreases in their homicide rate from year to year than states with a low rate of executions or no executions. This analysis supports Lester's results (though Wasserman denied this), but the analysis was more crude than Lester's analyses. Wasserman looked at the changes in the homicide rates from year to year for each state regardless of whether that state had executed anyone in a given year or not. Each state was simply classified as having a high rate of executions, a low rate, or none. The states with a high execution rate, for example, executed at least one person in about 80 percent of the years in the time period, and the states with a low execution rate executed at least one person in 28 percent of the years. For these states with a low execution rate, Wasserman looked at the number of decreases in the homicide rate overall, whereas Lester compared the changes in the homicide rate for the years after an execution year with those after a non-execution year.

Cloninger (1992) studied the states of America from 1983 to 1988 and looked at changes in the homicide rate from year to year in each state. Of the 254 one-period changes, in 34 at least one execution occurred in the state. Comparing these 34 changes with the remaining 220, Cloninger found that the executions had a deterrent effect on the homicide rate in the following year (an effect which was only marginally significant–that is, at the 8% level).

Lester (1989) examined monthly data published by Graves (1956) for three counties in California for 1946 to 1955. After months in which there was an execution, the homicide rate declined 61 percent of the time; for months in which there was no execution, the homicide rate declined only 50 percent of the time. This deterrent effect, however, was not statistically significant.

Does Watching an Execution Deter?

Espy (1980) searched historical accounts of murder and found cases of lawyers, sheriffs, and even hangmen who committed murders and were executed. He also found instances of relatives of hanged men who subsequently murdered others and were executed, even if they had watched the execution of their relatives? However, no quantitative data was presented on this issue.

Skyjackings

Chauncey (1975) found that after August, 1961, when execution was legalized for skyjacking, the number of attempted skyjackings in the next six months dropped as compared to the number in the prior six months (0 versus 5) and as compared to non-USA skyjackings (7 versus 4 for the same time periods).

A Mandatory Versus a Discretionary Death Penalty

Bowers (1974) compared states that switched from a mandatory to a discretionary death penalty with contiguous states that did not change and found no apparent difference in the murder rates.

Conclusions

The studies reviewed here provide support for the deterrent effect of the death penalty. Lester's and Wasserman's research indicate a deterrent effect from executions. However, Espy's cases show that a death penalty does not necessarily deter everyone.

REFERENCES

Bowers, W. *Executions in America.* Lexington, MA: D. C. Heath, 1974.

Chauncey, R. Deterrence, severity and skyjacking. *Criminology,* 1975, 12, 447-473.

Cloninger, D. O. Capital punishment and deterrence. *Applied Economics,* 1992, 24, 635-645.

Cochran, J. K., Chamlin, M. B., & Seth, M. Deterrence or brutalization? *Criminology,* 1994, 32, 107-134.

Espy, J. Capital punishment and deterrence. *Crime and Delinquency,* 1980, 26, 537-544.

Graves, W. A doctor looks at capital punishment. *Medical Arts and Sciences,* 1956, 10(4), 137-141.

Lester, D. Homicide and the death penalty. *Journal of the American Medical Association,* 1973, 225, 313.

Lester, D. Executions as a deterrent to homicides. *Psychological Reports,* 1979a, 44, 562.

Lester, D. Deterring effect on executions on murder as a function of number and proportion of executions. *Psychological Reports,* 1979b, 45, 598.

Lester, D. Effect of Gary Gilmore's execution on homicidal behavior. *Psychological Reports,* 1980, 57, 1262.

Lester, D. The deterrent effect of executions on homicide. *Psychological Reports,* 1989, 64, 306.

McFarland, S. Is capital punishment a short-term deterrent to homicide? *Journal of Criminal Law and Criminology,* 1983, 74, 1014-1032.

Wasserman, I. Non-deterrent effect of executions on homicide rates. *Psychological Reports,* 1981, 58, 137-138.

Chapter 11

REGIONAL CORRELATES OF THE DEATH PENALTY AND EXECUTION RATES

Although most research has focused on whether the presence of a death penalty in a region (or the number or rate of executions) is related to a decrease in the murder rate, a more general question explored by Lester and Yang in a series of studies is what social characteristics are associated with the presence of a death penalty in a state or the rate of executions.

Execution Rates

Yang and Lester (1988a) reanalyzed data reported by Cloninger (1977) for a cross-sectional analysis of execution rates in the American states for 1955 to 1959. During this period, 41 states had a death penalty. The social variables studied by Cloninger in his analysis of whether the execution rate deterred murder included the confinement rate of prisoners, the percentage of low-income families, the unemployment rate, the percentage of non-whites, the median age, the population size, and the population change from 1960 to 1962. In addition, Yang and Lester included the homicide rate in their reanalysis. Yang and Lester found that these variables accounted for only 23 percent of the variance (R^2) in the execution rate, with only median age giving a statistically significant regression coefficient.

In an effort to identify a better set of predictors of the execution rates of the 41 states with a death penalty, this time in 1955 to 1964, Yang and Lester (1988b) examined the predictive power of the murder rate, the rate of other violent crimes, the rate of property crime, the strictness of state handgun control laws, the innovativeness of state legislatures, and the percentage of state expenditures on welfare. These variables accounted for 45 percent of the variance (R^2) in the execution rates, an improvement over their previous study. Only the innovativeness of the state legislatures contributed significantly to the multiple regression. In a reanalysis of this data set, Yang and Lester (1990) found that the set of predictors was more successful in predicting the execution rate per capita ($R^2 = 0.52$) than the execution rate per murderer ($R^2 = 0.13$). In this reanalysis, only the murder rate contributed significantly to the prediction of the execution rate per capita.

Presence of a Death Penalty

In a preliminary study, Lester (1986) found that states which did not have a death penalty in 1980 had a lower overall crime rate, a lower murder rate and were in the north of the continental United States. The presence of a death penalty was not related to longitude, population, population density or to the Republican vote in the presidential election in 1980.

Yang and Lester compared the 41 states with a death penalty in 1955 to 1959 with the remaining states and found no differences in the confinement rate of prisoners, the percentage of low-income families, the unemployment rate, the percentage of non-whites, the median age, the population size or the population change from 1960 to 1962. The states with a death penalty did have higher homicide rates.

Yang and Lester (1989a) found that continental states in 1960 with no death penalty were characterized by larger populations, were less often in the South, and had lower violent crime rates (excluding murder). The two groups of states did not differ in the murder rate, the rate of property crime, the strictness of state handgun control laws, the innovativeness of state legislatures, the percentage vote for the Republican presidential candidate in 1960, the unemployment rate, the percentage of people with low incomes, the percentage of the state budget spent of welfare, the percentage of non-whites, the median age or the median school years completed.

Yang and Lester (1989b; Lester, 1994) sought to explore this question in a more systematic manner by applying a factor-analytic technique to a different and broader set of social characteristics than that used in the Yang and Lester study (1989a). The set of social variables was obtained from a larger data set for the 48 contiguous continental states in 1980 (Lester, 1994), and the variables are listed in Table 1, together with the results of a factor analysis (using SPSSX with a principal components extraction and a varimax rotation).

Table 1
RESULTS OF THE FACTOR ANALYSIS
(WITH DECIMAL POINTS OMITTED)

	Factor						
	I	II	III	IV	V	VI	VII
median family income	74#	−04	−01	−14	58#	08	−11
% urban	92#	09	−08	13	−01	−05	06
per capita income	79#	08	21	−14	48#	−07	−16
population	62#	−19	14	25	−16	18	−40
population density	54#	−38	37	11	08	07	44#
personal income	80#	14	23	−13	47#	−07	−13
% in poverty	−50#	−06	−13	47#	−54#	02	01
gross state product	42#	26	−28	−09	33	−29	−33
% immigrants	86#	08	23	−03	−10	01	18
% Roman Catholic	60#	−08	32	−32	16	06	45#
% born in state	−40#	−81#	05	07	−12	19	−12
crime rate	72#	53#	−01	17	05	05	15
divorce rate	−02	88#	−16	02	−03	−01	−08
interstate migration	−04	83#	−27	−10	11	−32	13
church attendance	−10	−73#	−20	−20	−19	−33	21
% divorced	15	91#	−08	−07	06	13	−16
gun control strictness	27	−58#	18	13	13	20	−08
alcohol consumption	31	53#	14	−16	39	−15	35
females/males	10	−50#	55#	34	−31	21	26
longitude	10	50#	−54#	−28	−07	−09	−38
birth rate	−14	11	−92#	−14	−12	−18	−10
% voting for Reagan	05	23	−58#	−33	−08	−45#	−05
% over 65 years	−05	−22	69#	−29	−51#	−20	−02
death rate	−10	−32	79#	−05	−43#	−01	−04
% under 15 years	−32	−05	−91#	−01	−12	06	02
median age	31	03	92#	−02	−15	−01	01
southern index	−26	27	−12	73#	−30	11	−34
% separated	26	−04	18	84#	12	14	15
% black	−10	−16	04	92#	−10	13	−01
latitude	02	−13	08	−77#	43#	16	05
infant mortality rate	05	−25	17	82#	−17	15	01
females in labor force	12	10	−02	−15	81#	−32	14
males in labor force	19	03	−34	−26	80#	−29	−01
employment ratio	03	08	−15	−20	75#	−47#	02
unemployment rate	01	−05	03	07	−20	96#	−01
male unemployment	07	−07	06	−07	−17	93#	−08
female unemployment	−06	−01	−03	27	−21	88#	12
% of variance	26%	21%	13%	8%	7%	5%	3%

= high loading (greater than 0.40)

Thirty-eight states had the death penalty for all or part of 1980, while ten did not have a death penalty. The presence of a death penalty was associated with the crime rate, male unemployment, the percentage born in-state, the percentage of young and elderly, the percentage separated, latitude, Southernness, the percentage of blacks, and the divorce rate (see Table 2).

Table 2
CORRELATIONS BETWEEN SOCIAL VARIABLES AND THE PRESENCE OF A DEATH PENALTY

	Point biserial r		Point biserial r
divorce rate	0.25*	latitude	-0.33*
interstate migration	0.32*	longitude	0.17
median family income	-0.08	alcohol consumption	0.11
% black	0.29*	death rate	-0.21
church attendance	-0.24	% under 15 years	0.10
% Roman Catholic	-0.15	% born in state	-0.36*
birth rate	0.14	% immigrants	0.13
% voting for Reagan	0.07	infant mortality rate	0.22
southern index	0.32*	median age	-0.06
% urban	0.17	% in poverty	0.23
% separated	0.41*	gross state product	0.09
% divorced	0.20	personal income	0.03
per capita income	-0.04	unemployment rate	-0.17
% over 65 years	-0.27*	male unemployment	-0.26*
females in labor force	0.01	female unemployment	0.01
males in labor force	0.01	employment ratio	0.06
gun control strictness	-0.06	crime rate	0.25*
population	0.09	females/males	-0.02
population density	-0.02		

* significant at the 5% level or better

Looking at factor scores, the presence of a death penalty was associated with scores on Factors II and IV (see Table 3). States with less social integration (high divorce and interstate migration rate and poor church attendance) and those in the South were more likely to have a death penalty.

Table 3
CORRELATIONS BETWEEN THE FACTOR SCORES
AND THE PRESENCE OF A DEATH PENALTY

Factor I	urban/wealth	0.10
Factor II	social disintegration	0.27*
Factor III	age	−0.14
Factor IV	southern	0.43*
Factor V	labor force participation	−0.03
Factor VI	unemployment	−0.17
Factor VII	Roman Catholicism	0.08

* significant at the 5% level or better

The results of both the present study and the earlier study by Yang and Lester indicate that the death penalty is more likely to be found in Southern states and in states where indices of social disintegration are higher.

Other Research

Mikesell and Pirog-Good (1990) used the presence of the death penalty in a state as an index of the severity of sanctions in the state and found that this variable did not predict higher property crime rates in the state. Harries (1988) found that, although murder and execution rates were highest in the Southern states, residents there in a national survey in 1977 rated the severity of an offense leading to the death of a victim lower than did residents of other regions.

Zimring (1990-1991) noted that execution rates were highest in the Southern states, but that a stronger predictor of 1980s execution rates was the execution rates of the states in the 1950s.

States differ considerably in other characteristics such as the percentage of death sentences commuted by state (Bedau, 1990-1991), state regulations concerning the provision and payment of lawyers for defendants (Wilson & Spangenberg, 1989), and the provision of mandatory death sentences for some offenses (Poulos, 1986), but no research has yet been conducted on the regional correlates of these variables.

REFERENCES

Bedau, H. A. The decline of executive clemency in capital cases. *New York University Review of Law and Social Change*, 1990-1991, 18, 255-272.

Cloninger, D. Deterrence and the death penalty. *Journal of Behavioral Economics*, 1977, 6, 87-105.

Harries, K. D. Regional variations in homicide, capital punishment, and perceived crime severity in the United States. *Geografiska Annaler*, 1988, 70B, 325-334.

Lester, D. *Which states have a death penalty?* Unpublished manuscript, 1986.

Lester, D. *Patterns of suicide and homicide in America.* Commack, NY: Nova Science, 1994.

Mikesell, J., & Pirog-Good, M. A. State lotteries and crime. *American Journal of Economics and Sociology*, 1990, 49, 7-19.

Poulos, J. W. The Supreme Court, capital punishment and the substantive criminal law. *Arizona Law Review*, 1986, 28, 143-257.

Wilson, R. J., & Spangenberg, R. L. State post-*Furman* representation of defendants sentenced to death. *Judicature*, 1989, 72, 331-337.

Yang, B., & Lester, D. Predicting execution rates in the USA. *Psychological Reports*, 1988a, 62, 305-306.

Yang, B., & Lester, D. A hypothesis about execution rates in the United States. *Proceedings of the 3rd Annual Meeting of the Pennsylvania Economic Association* (pp. 522-529). University Park: Pennsylvania State University, 1988b.

Yang, B., & Lester, D. Which states have a death penalty? *Psychological Reports*, 1989a, 64, 1180.

Yang, B., & Lester, D. Which states have the death penalty? *Psychological Reports*, 1989b, 65, 185-186.

Yang, B., & Lester, D. Predicting execution rates in the United States. *Psychological Reports*, 1990, 67, 1146.

Zimring, F. E. Ambivalence in state capital punishment policy. *New York University Review of Law and Social Change*, 1990-1991, 18, 729-742.

Chapter 12

OTHER ISSUES

A number of other issues on capital punishment have been raised, but little research has been conducted on them. This chapter briefly surveys these issues.

Murder as a Means to Suicide

If the sentence for murder is execution, then it has been argued that some people might murder as a means of completing suicide. Although cases have been reported of murderers who may have been motivated in part in their murder by the fact that they would be executed, which would constitute suicide by means of victim-precipitated murder (Lester & Lester, 1975), there has been no accurate documentation of this phenomenon.

Strafer (1983) noted that at least five of the eight men executed since 1976, at some point or another, volunteered to give in to the process leading to their execution. However, this may represent acceptance of the death sentence rather than a sign of suicidal motivation prior to the murder.

Rawlins (1976) devised an interesting technique to study the phenomenon. He compared murderers killing in states with a death penalty with those killing where there was no death penalty. They did not differ in guilt, overcontrol or overt expression of emotion on the Minnesota Multiphasic Personality Inventory. Thus, Rawlins could not conclude that a death penalty causes some people to murder in order to be executed.

The Death Penalty as an Inducement to Murder

It has been argued that, if murder receives a severe sentence, such as the death penalty, then murderers will commit further murders (especially of police officers) in order to escape capture.

Bailey (1982) looked at all of the states in the United States from 1961 to 1971 and worked out the rates with which police officers were killed in each state. For these eleven years, the abolition states had higher rates of police officers killed in six years and lower rates in five years. In a cross-sectional study, Bailey correlated the rate with which police officers were killed and the execution rate. For seven of the years (the only seven in which executions took place), five of the correlations were negative (indicating a deterrent effect) and two were positive, but none were statistically significant. When Bailey carried out the multiple regression with socio-demographic variables included, the contribution of executions was not significant.

Are Innocent People Executed?

MacNamara (1969) noted several cases of innocent men convicted and executed for murder but gives no accurate count of the frequency of this event and no comparable data on people innocent of murder, convicted and sentenced to life imprisonment.

Bedau and Radelet (1987) identified 350 cases of defendants convicted of capital or potentially capital crimes in this century who were later found or suspected to be innocent. Of these, 326 involved murder. One hundred and thirty-nine of the 350 people were sentenced to death, but only 23 executed. Only two of these 23 were executed since 1946, one in 1960 and one in 1974. Bedau and Radelet estimated that between 1900 and 1942, 0.36 percent of the sample had been executed; between 1943 and 1985, 0.22 percent. However, their choice of 1942/1943 as the dividing point seems to have been chosen in order to include two executions which took place in 1945 in the second time period.

Although innocent people have been executed for crimes they did not commit, there is by no means universal acceptance that all of the people on Bedau and Radelet's list of 23 executions were innocent. For some, there may be doubt about their guilt, but there remains some evidence supporting their guilt.

Markman and Cassell (1988) criticized this report since (1) only 7 percent of the cases involved possibly erroneous executions, (2) Bedau and Radelet misrepresented the circumstances of several of the cases, and (3) Bedau and Radelet ignored recent safeguards which make execution of the innocent very unlikely today.

Are Murderers Likely to Murder Again?

It has been argued that murderers very rarely murder again. Thus, it is not necessary to execute them to protect society from them. Is this true?

Giardini and Farrow (1952) surveyed 22 states for a period of one to 38 years. He found that, of 197 capital cases paroled, only 11.7 percent violated parole (and only 5.6 percent violated parole by committing another offense). However, no control data were presented from other offenders.

Stanton (1969) studied 63 murderers convicted of first-degree murder and 514 murderers convicted of second-degree murder. After parole, only three of the first-degree murderers violated parole as compared to 115 of the second-degree murderers (two of whom murdered). He noted that the first-degree murderers were a selected (non-random) group since, during the period studied, 327 other first-degree murderers were executed.

In a second study, 7 percent of murderers were reconvicted for crimes after parole as compared to 20 percent of other criminals. Thus, their general recidivism rate (for any crime) was lower. Stanton noted that paroled murderers were older than the other convicts (45 versus 26 on the average), had been in prison longer (15 years versus 28 months on the average), but had fewer prior felonies. A further study of parolees also found a lower parole violation rate for murderers.

Lehtinen (1977) cited data from an unpublished NAACP study showing that two paroled murderers out of 994 were imprisoned subsequently for murder. However, no specific data were given on how many years they had been at risk for murder.

Sellin (1980) reported data on paroled prisoners and found that the rate of murder among parolees was not the highest for murderers. They ranked sixth out of sixteen crimes for committing murder during the first three years after parole.

Vito and Wilson (1988) looked at 23 inmates on death row in Kentucky who had their sentences voided after the *Furman* decision. Seventeen were paroled, three of whom violated parole and four committed new crimes. Thirty-five percent were rearrested and 29 percent convicted. However, these investigators did not study a comparison group.

Marquart and Sorensen (1988) compared 47 *Furman* inmates whose death sentences were commuted with 156 men sentenced to life imprisonment in Texas. The two groups did not differ in rule infractions while in prison. Sixty-four percent of the *Furman* inmates were released versus 70 percent of the lifers. The recidivism rates were similar (25% and 17%) and the felony arrest rates (14% and 6%). One of the *Furman* offenders committed a new murder versus none of the lifers. The lifers spent longer in prison than the *Furman* inmates, but they did not differ in offense, race, age, prior violent offenses or prior incarcerations. Thus, those offenders whose death sentences were commuted did not differ significantly from the life-imprisonment inmates in later years.

Marquart et al. (1989) compared inmates sentenced to death in Texas from 1974 to 1988 and whose sentences were commuted or reversed with murderers sentenced to life imprisonment. The two groups did not differ significantly in prior criminal record, the type of murder, institutional behavior, and, if released, recidivism.

Marquart and Sorensen (1989) studied 558 inmates whose death sentences were commuted after the *Furman* ruling by the United States Supreme Court in 1972. Over the next fifteen years, about 30 percent committed serious prison rule violations, including six murders, but Marquart and Sorensen do not give data on a comparable group (say, of murderers initially sentenced to prison terms). For 243 inmates released from prison, after 1,282 years in the community, 52 had returned to prison, but only one had committed murder.

The Relative Financial Cost

Rarely are data provided to compare the cost of executions and life imprisonment, though the relative cost is often used as an argument for or against the death penalty.

Nakell (1978) discussed the relative costs of executions versus life imprisonment, but gave no firm figures. Anderson (1983) estimated prison costs at $30,000 per year for 50 years, which comes to $1.5 million. A capital punishment case costs about $176,000 for defense costs, $845,000 for the prosecution and $300,000 for court costs. This comes to $1.5 million. However, Anderson forgot that there are defense, prosecution and court costs for non-capital murder trials, too. The critical costs are the appeals process above and beyond the normal appeals process and the costs of the execution versus life imprisonment. Anderson did not present any data on these costs. Thus, there are still no comparative data on the relative costs of the two processes.

Furthermore, those who write on this topic typically fail to distinguish between fixed costs (for example, judges get their salary regardless of which case they are hearing) and additional costs. They also fail to take into account factors such as those discussed by Viscuso (1994) in his analysis of the cost of smoking. Viscuso noted that the premature deaths caused by smoking save a great deal of money from the elimination of health care costs, medical treatments, nursing home care and pension and social security benefits. Viscuso concluded that each pack of cigarettes sold saves more money than it costs to purchase. Those who attempt to estimate the relative costs of a death sentence versus imprisonment need to invite sound economists and individuals on both sides of the issue.

The Act of Executing

Turnbull (1978) argued that the act of execution is cruel and inhumane. He pointed out that the four major methods are painful to the person executed, mutilating, and horrifying to witnesses. Hanging, shooting, gassing and electrocution each have barbarous elements–in none is death instantaneous, for example–and all lead to heightened fear and horror for the condemned person as the equipment is readied. Turnbull noted that death by injection may be the least cruel of the methods for execution. No research has appeared in which people have rated the cruelty of the different methods of execution.

Haines (1989) has discussed the ethical issues in having physicians act as executioners when the method of execution is a lethal injection. Since an injection appears to be a quasi-medical procedure, there is the option of having a skilled physician perform this task, but it may conflict with the motives for becoming a physician and with the Hippocratic oath that physicians take.

In a more detailed examination of the ways in which executions are carried out (and are flawed), Haines (1992) examined media reports of executions and found that the most frequent flaw was that the execution was botched in some way and the prisoner did not die quickly and painlessly as planned. The prisoner did not always play his assigned role, and the solemnity of the death chamber was violated (as when a prisoner was abused). Looking at public reaction, the most common complaint was that there were irregularities in the conviction and sentencing of the prisoner.

Who Is Affected by an Execution?

In an earlier chapter, it was noted that little research has been conducted on the effects of death row on people. However, there are many other individuals involved who might legitimately be studied: the victim, the significant others of the victim and the murderer, the police, the prosecutor, the judge and jurors, the guards and prison wardens, fellow prisoners, and the executioner. Recently, Kaplan (1985) wrote about the stress on jurors, but he did conduct a quantitative study on their stress.

Freinkel et al. (1994) questioned fifteen media persons who witnessed an execution. They found that the average number of items related to having dissociative symptoms endorsed was 5.0 and for anxiety items 3.9, similar to scores of people who witnessed catastrophes such as fire storms. The number of anxiety items endorsed was positively associated with the number of dissociative items endorsed, and Freinkel concluded that the responses indicated that witnessing the execution was quite traumatic for the witnesses.

The Retarded and Juveniles

Although the United States Supreme Court has not barred the execution of mentally retarded offenders, there has been much debate as to the appropriateness of executing the retarded, as well as juveniles (Baroff, 1991), especially since mental retardation and youth may be relevant to judgments about personal blameworthiness.

However, the United States Supreme Court has ruled that it is unconstitutional to execute an offender who is mentally incompetent (*Ford v. Wainwright*, 1986). Susman (1992) explored different criteria for evaluating such incompetence and found that they produced differed decisions. Deitchman (1992) found that forensic examiners (psychiatrists and psychologists) who were in favor of the death penalty were more likely to judge a hypothetical clinically ambiguous death row inmate as competent to be executed than examiners opposed to the death penalty.

Historical Studies

Mackesy (1993) studied capital cases at the Old Bailey in London (England) from 1782 to 1783. In 166 cases, 58 people were executed and 108 pardoned. The pardons were primarily made to correct prosecutorial abuses, to prevent injustices and to discourage some kinds of crimes more than others. There did seem to be an effort to "make the punishment fit the crime."

Lynching and Executions

Several studies have examined the association between lynching and executions in the past. Phillips (1987) studied North Carolina from 1889 to 1918 and found that, although fewer whites were executed or lynched than blacks, there was no association between ethnic group and outcome (execution versus lynching). For blacks only, from 1889 to 1903 the numbers of executions and the numbers of lynchings each year were positively associated, but from 1903 to 1918 there was no significant association.

Massey and Myers (1989) studied Georgia from 1882 to 1935 and found that the lynching, execution and incarceration rates for blacks were not significantly associated.

Conclusions

The issues discussed in this chapter are important issues and deserve more empirical attention than they have received in the past. The innocence of some executed offenders, the likelihood of death row inmates murdering again if they were released, and the impact on those involved in capital murder and executions need to be examined in greater depth using sound methodological techniques.

More needs to be explored about the relative financial costs of life imprisonment versus a death sentence primarily because this issue, regardless of its relevance, is frequently raised in discussions about capital punishment. A sound discussion, however, needs advocates for both sides of the capital punishment debate who would raise costs for the other's side and dispute costs raised by their opponents. In addition, well-trained economists who have addressed similar issues, such as Viscuso, should be included in the panel.

REFERENCES

Anderson, K. An eye for an eye. *Time*, 1983, 121(4), 28-39.

Bailey, W. Capital punishment and lethal assaults against police. *Criminology*, 1982, 19, 608-625.

Baroff, G. S. Establishing mental retardation in capital cases. *Mental Retardation*, 1991, 29, 343-349.

Bedau, H. A., & Radelet, M. Miscarriages of justice in potentially capital cases. *Stanford Law Review*, 1987, 40, 21-179.

Deitchman, M. A. Factors affecting competency-for-execution decision-making in Florida forensic examiners. *Dissertation Abstracts International*, 1992, 52B, 6080.

Ford v. Wainwright [106 S.Ct. 2595 (1986)].

Freinkel, A., Koopman, C., & Spiegel, D. Dissociative symptoms in media eyewitnesses of an execution. *American Journal of Psychiatry*, 1994, 151, 1335-1339.

Giardini, G., & Farrow, R. The paroling of capital offenders. *Annals of the American Academy of Political and Social Science*, 1952, #284, 85-94.

Haines, H. Primum non nocere. *Social Problems*, 1989, 36, 442-454.

Haines, H. Flawed execution, the anti-death penalty movement, and the politics of capital punishment. *Social Problems*, 1992, 39, 125-138.

Kaplan, S. M. Death, so they say. *Psychology Today*, 1985, 19(7), 48-53.

Lehtinen, M. The value of life. *Crime and Delinquency*, 1979, 23, 237-252.

Lester, D., & Lester, G. *Crime of passion.* Chicago: Nelson-Hall, 1975.

Mackesy, R. Lethal lottery or coherent scheme? *Dissertation Abstracts International*, 1993, 54A, 1551.

MacNamara, D. Convicting the innocent. *Crime and Delinquency*, 1969, 15, 57-61.

Markman, S. J., & Cassell, P. G. Protecting the innocent. *Stanford Law Review*, 1988, 41, 121-160.

Marquart, J. W., Ekland-Olson, S., & Sorensen, J. R. Gazing into the crystal ball. *Law and Society Review*, 1989, 23, 449-468.

Marquart, J. W., & Sorensen, J. R. Institutional and post-release behavior of *Furman*-commuted inmates in Texas. *Criminology*, 1988, 26, 677-693.

Marquart, J. W., & Sorensen, J. R. A national study of the *Furman*-commuted inmates. *Loyola of Los Angeles Law Review*, 1989, 23, 5-28.

Massey, J. L., & Myers, M. A. Patterns of repressive social control in post-reconstruction Georgia, 1882-1935. *Social Forces*, 1989, 68, 458-488.

Nakell, B. The cost of the death penalty. *Criminal Law Bulletin*, 1978, 14(1), 69-80.

Phillips, C. D. Exploring relations among forms of social control. *Law and Society Review*, 1987, 21, 361-374.

Rawlins, G. An exploratory study of some psychological implications of the death penalty as measured on the MMPI of convicted murderers. *Dissertation Abstracts International*, 1976, 36B, 5813-5814.

Sellin, T. *The penalty of death*. Beverly Hills, CA: Sage, 1980.

Stanton, J. Murderers on parole. *Crime and Delinquency*, 1969, 15, 149-155.

Strafer, G. Volunteering for execution. *Journal of Criminal Law and Criminology*, 1983, 74, 860-912.

Susman, D. T. Effect of three different legal standards on psychologists' determinations of competence for execution. *Dissertation Abstracts International*, 1992, 53B, 1619.

Turnbull, C. Death by decree. *Natural History*, 1978, 87(5), 51-66.

Viscuso, W. K. *Cigarette taxation and the social consequences of smoking*. Cambridge, MA: NBER, 1994.

Vito, G. F., & Wilson, D. G. Back from the dead. *Justice Quarterly*, 1988, 5, 101-111.

Chapter 13

CONCLUSIONS

Several features of the research on capital punishment are notewor-thy. First, there is little research on some of the issues. There is virtually no research at all on life on death row as compared to other parts of the prison. There is virtually no research on the type of person who is on death row and who gets executed. Although a few studies have looked at socio-demographic differences between those who are executed and those who are sentenced to life imprisonment, no sound psychological studies have appeared.

Second, many studies are methodologically unsound. For example, investigators have documented cases of innocent men executed for murder. They have not, however, studied a control group of innocent men sentenced to imprisonment for murder. Studies on the psychoneurological characteristics of death row inmates have not examined the same characteristics in non-death row inmates.

Third, the emotions associated with the death penalty have influenced, not only the research itself, but the interpretation of the results of the research by investigators. Investigators will present results, say, on deterrence, which are mixed and then draw a conclusion in line with their own personal opinion. A researcher will use a "facts and myths" inventory to measure knowledge about capital punishment in which the "facts" are clearly "myths" to a researcher with different opinions. Journal policies add to this bias. I have in my files copies of sound papers by other authors showing, for example, a deterrent effect of capital punishment but which were rejected by sociological and criminal justice journals which have published articles purporting to find no deterrent effect. In one case, a journal agreed to publish an article showing a deterrent effect on condition the journal included a criticism of the research (which added nothing to the debate), while not adhering to the same policy for articles purporting to show no deterrent effect.

Fourth, often the investigators show a lack of logic in the conclusions they draw from their research. For example, the fact that discrimination by race, gender, age and social class may play a role in the sentencing for capital murder is not necessarily an argument against the death penalty. It is an argument against discrimination. Discrimination in public transport, housing or restaurants did not lead to the elimination of buses, houses or restaurants. It lead to efforts to eliminate the discrimination.

This does not mean, of course, that I will be any different in this chapter. However, I will do my best to draw conclusions from the research fairly and make clear my own prejudices when I draw inferences.

The Findings

The death penalty does seem to have become less prevalent (and less barbaric) in modern times. It is noteworthy that modern industrialized nations are less likely to have a death penalty than less developed nations, and that over the course of history the death penalty has been eliminated for many crimes in some nations.

Data on those sentenced to be executed for murder does shown an underrepresentation of females, an overrepresentation of blacks, and a typical offender who is poorly educated, young and single. However, such a description does not have implications until we know how many murderers are male, black, poorly educated, young and single. Furthermore, these characteristics cannot necessarily be used to excuse the murderers. There are psychologists and psychiatrists who see few characteristics, if any, as excuses for behavior (see, for example, Glasser, 1965). Not all blacks, not all males, and not all poorly educated people turn to a life of crime or murder.

Research on the perceived severity of the death penalty is surprising. Members of the general public rate life imprisonment as close in severity to execution. This is reasonable since many published accounts of life in prison describe it as horrendous.

Studies of those on death row are rare. The only quantitative findings are that murder and suicide rates are high on death row.

The research into attitudes toward the death penalty is hard to summarize. Not only is this one of the most researched issues, it is also the issue with the least relevance to social policy. My feeling is that the topic is studied so much because it is easy to carry out research. The conclusions of the review in Chapter 6 were that support for capital punishment was stronger in older people, the less educated, those earning more, whites, and those with conservative and authoritarian attitudes. The more interesting research has appeared since the last edition of this book–research which showed that the wording of the questions on capital punishment had a great impact on the respondents' responses. For example, support for the death penalty was less if the respondents were presented with life imprisonment without parole as an option. However, the policy implications of these findings must be tempered by the fact that a sentence to life imprisonment without parole does not guarantee that laws and rules will not be changed in the future, permitting these "lifers" freedom.

Discrimination, Juries and the Death Penalty

Early studies on whether blacks are more likely to be executed than whites showed that blacks were more likely to be executed. For example, most of the executions for the crime of rape were of blacks in the South. Modern research, using much more sound methodologies, occasionally shows discrimination persisting in modern times, but it is the race of the *victim* that appears most relevant. Murderers of white victims are more likely to be sentenced to death than murderers of black victims. In the years after the *Furman* decision, a few studies have found that white murderers are more likely to be sentenced to death and executed than black murderers. However, race is not the only extraneous variable that has been found to affect decision making in the criminal justice system. For example, Bowers (1983) found that the region of the state in which the trial took place and the type of attorney representing the defendant were also relevant to the outcome.

Studies of juries have found that the knowledge that a guilty verdict may result in a death penalty appears to have an impact on jury decisions of guilt versus innocence. Other research indicates that elimination of jurors with particular attitudes does bias the verdicts given by the juries. However, jurors may be removed from the jury pool and challenged for a wide range of factors, and so the criminal justice system never employs a random selection of jurors from the jury pool.

This research raises serious questions, but not just about the processing of murder trials by the criminal justice system. It raises questions about the criminal justice system, especially about the ability of juries as presently constituted in the United States to render just verdicts. My personal opinion is that jury trials are a poor way of deciding upon guilt and sentences. The decisions of juries are of unparalleled importance in determining the future lives of defendants and offenders. Yet, we permit these decisions to be made by people with no formal education or training in the criminal justice field. It is as if we said that surgery could be carried out by any group of our peers. The fact that juries are affected by factors other than the circumstances of the crime should come as no surprise.

Does the Death Penalty Deter?

This of course is the critical issue that could be decided by social scientists. However, as we have seen in Chapter 9, the conclusions which can be drawn from the research are far from clear.

Time-Series Studies

In 19 studies (or substudies) looking at the United States as a whole over some period between 1930 and the present, ten have reported a deterrent effect in at least some analyses (Bechdoldt, 1977; Bowers & Pierce, 1975; Cantor & Cohen, 1980; Chressanthis, 1989; Cover & Thistle, 1988; Ehrlich, 1975; Hoenack & Weiler, 1980; Layson, 1985; Passell & Taylor, 1977; Yunker, 1976/1977), three studies found a brutalization effect (Bowers & Pierce, 1975; Shin, 1978; Yunker, 1976/1977), while six found no significant effects (Bechdoldt, 1977; Bowers & Pierce, 1975; Kleck, 1979; Passell & Taylor, 1977; Shin, 1978; Yunker 1976/1977). The results are clearly quite mixed.

As we pointed out above, although Ehrlich's classic study was a vast methodological improvement over the research that had appeared before, it makes little sense. It is methodologically unsound to look at the United States as a whole. Some states did not have a death penalty, and other states executed virtually no murders. Time-series studies must be carried out on individual states (or cities).

In time-series studies of individual states or cities, nine studies have found no significant effect (Bailey, 1978a, 1978b, 1979a, 1979b, 1979c,

1983a, 1984a; Decker & Kohfeld, 1984, 1987), one found a brutalization effect (Bowers & Pierce, 1980) and one found a deterrent effect (Decker & Kohfeld, 1984).

However, Bailey (1979-1980) carried out time-series analyses in 37 states. He found a deterrent effect in 24, a brutalization effect in eight and zero effect in five. This study is clearly the superior study in the literature since it included as many states as possible, rather than selecting a possibly unrepresentative state. The results do seem to suggest a weak deterrent effect from the death penalty, since the deterrent effect is found more often than the brutalization effect or no effect.

In Canada, two studies have reported a deterrent effect (Avio, 1988; Layson, 1983) while two have reported no significant effect (Avio, 1979; Lester, 1993). Wolpion (1978) reported a deterrent effect for England and Wales.

Cross-Sectional Studies

In cross-section studies of the United States, six studies found no significant effect (Bailey, 1977; Bailey, 1980b; Black & Orsagh, 1978; Boyes & McPheters, 1977; Passell, 1975; Shin, 1978), five found a deterrent effect (Bailey, 1974, Bailey, 1975; Cloninger, 1977/1987; Veall, 1992; Yang & Lester, 1988), six found a brutalization effect (Bailey, 1976; Bailey, 1980b; Bechdoldt, 1977; Black & Orsagh, 1978; Ehrlich, 1977; Glaser & Ziegler, 1974), and one found mixed results (Peterson & Bailey, 1988). Bailey (1983b) found no association between changes in the homicide rate and changes in the execution rate from 1950 to 1960.

Again, it was Bailey (1980a) who carried out the best study. Rather than using one year (typically 1950 or 1960 in most of the studies), he carried out the cross-sectional study for every year from 1920 to 1962. Twenty years gave a deterrent effect, seven a brutalization effect and one a zero effect. Again, as in his time-series studies using states, the deterrent effect is found more often.

Thus, the evidence from the two major studies, as I identify them, both by Bailey, suggest that a deterrent effect exists.

It would be interesting in future research to search for reasons why some states and why some years give a deterrent effect while other do not. Such research would increase our understanding of the circumstances under which a deterrent effect might appear.

Publicity and Short-Term Effects

Six studies on the effects of media publicity of executions on the murder rate have reported a deterrent effect (Phillips, 1980; Phillips & Hensley, 1984; Stack, 1987, 1990, 1995; Stack & Gundlach, 1991), seven have reported no significant effect (Bailey, 1984b, 1990; Bailey & Peterson, 1989; Bullock, 1992; Grogger, 1990; King, 1978; Savitz, 1958), one a brutalization effect (Stack, 1993) and one mixed results (Peterson & Bailey, 1991).

Comment

I read the evidence as showing the possible existence of a weak deterrent effect from executions on murder. This deterrent effect is found, it might be noted, with only a small proportion of murderers being executed. The impact of a larger proportion of executions cannot be determined at the present time.

Conclusions

What should our social policy be about capital punishment? It is not the place of social science to determine social policy about any issue. The research conducted by social scientists may be relevant to social policy, but social policy is determined by many factors other than the results of research. Typically, social policy is a compromise between various extreme positions or competing principles.

Social science has been extremely useful in the death penalty controversy in documenting the influence of factors other than guilt or the circumstances of the murder in the decision to execute a murderer. It has also been useful in its efforts to document whether there is a deterrent value to the death penalty. How we let the results of the research influence our opinions is a matter of personal choice.

REFERENCES

Avio, K. Capital punishment in Canada. *Canadian Journal of Economics*, 1979, 12, 647-676.

Avio, K. Measurement errors and capital punishment. *Applied Economics*, 1988, 20, 1253-1262.

Bailey, W. Murder and the death penalty. *Journal of Criminal Law and Criminology*, 1974, 65, 416-423.

Bailey, W. Murder and capital punishment. *American Journal of Orthopsychiatry*, 1975, 45, 669-688.

Bailey, W. Use of the death penalty versus outrage at murder. *Crime and Delinquency*, 1976, 22, 31-39.

Bailey, W. Imprisonment versus the death penalty as a deterrent to murder. *Law and Human Behavior*, 1977, 1, 239-260.

Bailey, W. C. An analysis of the deterrent effect of the death penalty in North Carolina. *North Carolina Central Law Journal*, 1978a, 10, 29-49.

Bailey, W. C. Deterrence and the death penalty for murder in Utah. *Journal of Contemporary Law*, 1978b, 5, 1-20.

Bailey, W. The deterrent effect of the death penalty for murder in California. *Southern California Law Review*, 1979a, 52, 743-764.

Bailey, W. The deterrent effect of the death penalty for murder in Ohio. *Cleveland State Law Review*, 1979b, 28, 51-70.

Bailey, W. C. Deterrence and the death penalty for murder in Oregon. *Williamette Law Review*, 1979c, 16, 67-85.

Bailey, W. Deterrent effect of the death penalty. *Omega*, 1979-1980, 10, 235-259.

Bailey, W. A multivariate cross-sectional analysis of the deterrent effect of the death penalty. *Sociology and Social Research*, 1980a, 64, 183-207.

Bailey, W. Deterrence and the celerity of the death penalty. *Social Forces*, 1980b, 58, 1308-1333.

Bailey, W. Disaggregation in deterrence and death penalty research. *Journal of Criminal Law and Criminology*, 1983a, 74, 827-859.

Bailey, W. C. The deterrent effect of capital punishment during the 1950s. *Suicide and Life-Threatening Behavior*, 1983b, 13, 95-107.

Bailey W. C. Murder and capital punishment in the nation's capital. *Justice Quarterly*, 1984a, 1, 211-223.

Bailey, W. C. Disaggregation in deterrence and death penalty research. *Journal of Criminal Law and Criminology*, 1984b, 74, 827-859.

Bailey, W. C. Murder, capital punishment, and television. *American Sociological Review*, 1990, 55, 628-637.

Bailey, W. C., & Peterson, R. D. Murder and capital punishment. *American Sociological Review*, 1989, 54, 722-743.

Bailey, W. C., & Peterson, R. D. Capital punishment and non-capital cases. *Albany Law Review*, 1990, 54, 681-707.

Bechdoldt, B. Capital punishment and homicide rape rates in the US. *Journal of Behavioral Economics*, 1977, 6, 33-66.

Black, T., & Orsagh, T. New evidence on the efficacy of sanctions as a deterrent to homicide. *Social Science Quarterly*, 1978, 58, 616-631.

Bowers, W. The pervasiveness of arbitrariness and discrimination under post-*Furman* capital statutes. *Journal of Criminal Law and Criminology*, 1983, 74, 1067-1100.

Bowers, W., & Pierce, G. The illusion of deterrence in Isaac Ehrlich's research on capital punishment. *Yale Law Journal*, 1975, 85, 187-208.

Bowers, W., & Pierce, G. Deterrence or brutalization? *Crime and Delinquency*, 1980, 26, 453-484.

Boyes, W., & McPheters, L. Capital punishment as a deterrent to violent crime. *Journal of Behavioral Economics*, 1977, 6, 67-86.

Bullock, C. A. The effect of executions on homicides. *Dissertation Abstracts International*, 1992, 52A, 3733.

Cantor, D., & Cohen, L. Comparing measures of homicide trends. *Social Science Research*, 1980, 9, 121-145.

Chressanthis, G. A. Capital punishment and the deterrent effect. *Journal of Behavioral Economics*, 1989, 18(2), 81-97.

Cloninger, D. Deterrence and the death penalty. *Journal of Behavioral Economics*, 1977, 6, 87-105.

Cloninger, D. O. Capital punishment and deterrence. *Journal of Behavioral Economics*, 1987, 16(4), 55-57.

Cover, J. P., & Thistle, P. D. Time-series, homicide, and the deterrent effect of capital punishment. *Southern Economic Journal*, 1988, 54, 615-622.

Decker, S. H., & Kohfeld, C. W. A deterrence study of the death penalty in Illinois, 1933-1980. *Journal of Criminal Justice*, 1984, 12, 367-377.

Decker, S. H., & Kohfeld, C. W. An empirical analysis of the effect of the death penalty in Missouri. *Journal of Crime and Justice*, 1987, 10(1), 23-46.

Ehrlich, I. The deterrent effect of capital punishment. *American Economic Review*, 1975, 65, 397-417.

Ehrlich, I. Capital punishment and deterrence. *Journal of Political Economy*, 1977, 85, 741-788.

Glaser, D., & Ziegler, M. Use of the death penalty versus outrage at murder. *Crime and Delinquency*, 1974, 20, 333-338.

Glasser, W. *Reality Therapy*. New York: Harper & Row, 1965.

Grogger, J. The deterrent effect of capital punishment. *Journal of the American Statistical Association*, 1990, 85, 295-303.

Hoenack, S. A., & Weiler, W. C. A structural model of murder behavior and the criminal justice system. *American Economic Review*, 1980, 70, 327-344.

King, D. The brutalization effect. *Social Forces*, 1978, 57, 683-687.

Kleck, G. Capital punishment, gun ownership and homicide. *American Journal of Sociology*, 1979, 84, 882-910.

Layson, S. K. Homicide and deterrence. *Canadian Journal of Economics*, 1983, 16, 52-73.

Layson, S. K. Homicide and deterrence. *Southern Economic Journal*, 1985, 52, 68-89.

Lester, D. The deterrent effect of the death penalty in Canada. *Perceptual and Motor Skills*, 1993, 77, 186.

Passell, P. The deterrent effect of the death penalty. *Stanford Law Review*, 1975, 28, 61-80.

Passell, P., & Taylor, J. The deterrent effect of capital punishment. *American Economic Review*, 1977, 67, 445-451.

Peterson, R. D., & Bailey, W. C. Murder and capital punishment in the evolving context of the post-*Furman* era. *Social Forces*, 1988, 66, 774-807.

Peterson, R. D., & Bailey, W. C. Felony murder and capital punishment. *Criminology*, 1991, 29, 367-395.

Phillips, D. The deterrent effect of capital punishment. *American Journal of Sociology*, 1980, 86, 139-148.

Phillips, D., & Hensley, J. When violence is rewarded or punished. *Journal of Communication*, 1984, 34(3), 101-116.

Savitz, L. A study in capital punishment. *Journal of Criminal Law, Criminology and Police Science*, 1958, 49, 338-341.

Shin, K. *Death penalty and crime.* Fairfax, VA: George Mason University, 1978.

Stack, S. Publicized executions and homicide, 1950-1980. *American Sociological Review*, 1987, 52, 532-540.

Stack, S. Execution publicity and homicide in South Carolina. *Sociological Quarterly*, 1990, 31, 599-611.

Stack, S. Execution publicity and homicide in Georgia. *American Journal of Criminal Justice*, 1993, 18, 25-39.

Stack, S. The impact of publicized executions on homicide. *Criminal Justice and Behavior*, 1995, 22, 172-186.

Stack, S., & Gundlach, J. Execution publicity and homicide, 1940-1986. American Sociological Association meeting, Cincinnati, 1991.

Veall, M. R. Bootstrapping and the process of model selection. *Journal of Applied Econometrics*, 1992, 7, 93-99.

Wolpion, K. Capital punishment and homicide in England. *American Economic Review*, 1978, 68(2), 422-427.

Yang, B., & Lester, D. The deterrent effect of executions on murder. *Perceptual and Motor Skills*, 1988, 67, 878.

Yunker, J. Is the death penalty a deterrent to homicide? *Journal of Behavioral Economics*, 1976, 5, 45-82.

Yunker, J. Is the death penalty a deterrent to homicide? *Journal of Behavioral Economics*, 1977, 6, 361-397.

Appendix 1

ATTITUDES TOWARD THE DEATH PENALTY

DAVID LESTER

ABSTRACT: Two scales for measuring attitudes toward capital punishment were devised and their use explored. Attitudes appeared to be similar in police officers and students and unrelated to sex.

STUDY ONE

To explore how people feel about capital punishment, a questionnaire was devised, listing 20 criminal acts (see Table 1) and respondents were asked to check which deserved execution. The list was given to 67 police officers in training seminars (mean age 35.4 yr, SD = 6.3) and 70 college students in classes aged 18 to 22 years (mean age 19.0 yr, SD = 1.0).

Police officers checked an average of 10.7 of the acts and college students 8.6. An examination of the crimes which most often led to a recommendation of execution shows a similar ranking of seriousness of the crimes for both police officers and college students (see Table 1). The six crimes most deserving of execution according to both groups are: a person who assassinates the President of the U.S.A., a person who murders several people at different points in time, a person who tortures the victim before killing him/her, a person who kills several people at once, the murderer of a police officer, and a person who kills someone else's child.

For the police officers, there were no significant differences in the number of acts checked as appropriate for execution between state and municipal police officers ($t = 1.01$, $df = 62$). The number of acts checked was not related to their reasons for becoming police officers (classified as for pay and security, helping others, and power status)

(Lester, 1983), their desire for thrills, Type A personality, age, years of work, prior military service, height, weight or ectomorphy scores.

For the college students, there was no sex difference in the number of acts checked as appropriate for execution (phi coefficient = 0.11). Using the college student sample, an attempt was made to devise the best Guttman scale. It had five items, a coefficient of reproductibilty of 0.94 and a coefficient of scalability of 0.73. The items were 5, 14, 3, 16, 18.

The students were also administered the attitude toward rape scale of Feild (1978). The number of crimes suitable for execution was related to advocating a severe punishment for rape ($r = 0.29$, df = 69, $p < 0.01$), but not to the other scales.

STUDY TWO

Fifteen items (see Table 2) to measure attitudes toward capital punishment were put into a Likert-type format and administered to 90 students (mean age 23.5 yr, SD = 5.2). The responses were factor-analyzed using BMD03M from the BIOMED statistical package. Six factors were identified, four of which were interpretable: factor I as pro-rehabilitation (items 1, 3, 5, 9, and 13), factor II as executions are a deterrent (items 2 and 8), factor III as punishment should fit the criminal (items 11 and 12), and factor IV as life imprisonment is cruel (items 7 and 10).

There were no sex differences on factors II, III, and IV, but males scored lower on factor I ($r = -0.25$, $p < 0.05$). Seventy-one of the subjects also completed the Feild (1978) attitude toward rape scale and checked which of 9 crimes they saw as deserving a death penalty (murder, rape, kidnapping, political assassination, espionage, child abuse resulting in death, mass murderer, a person who has murdered more than once, and murder of a child. The only factor giving a significant correlation for both sexes with the number of crimes deserving execution was factor I ($r = -0.62$, $p < 0.01$), and no factor correlated significantly the pro-rape score from Feild's attitude scale.

Discussion

Two scales to measure attitudes toward capital punishment were devised, and their use illustrated here. Approval of capital punishment appears to be relatively independent of such variables as occupation and sex. Those who are in favor of capital punishment also approve of severe punishment for the crime of rape.

Table 1

Crime	Percent Advocating Execution	
	Police Officers	*College Students*
1. A person who shoots a bank teller while robbing a bank.	88%	56%
2. His/her partner who says "Shoot him/her" before the shot is fired.	51%	29%
3. A person who murders a spouse in the middle of an angry argument.	14%	27%
4. A person who assassinates the President of the USA.	94%	79%
5. A person who murders someone else's child.	97%	81%
6. A person who kills a police officer.	98%	79%
7. A person who murders several people at different points in time.	98%	79%
8. A person who tortures the victim before killing him/her.	97%	84%
9. A person who is psychotic and kills someone because he/she hears a voice telling him/her to do so.	42%	21%
10. A person who kills several people at once, as in a bomb explosion or in setting-fire to a building.	94%	71%
11. A person who commits treason in a time of war.	52%	30%
12. A person who commits treason in a time of peace.	27%	23%
13. A person who brutally rapes another person, where the victim played no role in precipitating the assault.	57%	44%
14. A parent who "accidentally" kills their own child as a result of child abuse.	37%	37%
15. A person with a long history of brutal assaults, but who has never killed anyone.	29%	14%
16. A person who kills another, but who is drunk at the time.	34%	20%
17. A hit-and-run driver who kills a pedestrian.	6%	30%
18. A person who kidnaps someone for ransom, but who doesn't physically harm the person.	15%	4%
19. A person who kidnaps someone for ransom and physically harms (but does not kill) the victim.	23%	30%
20. A soldier who commits atrocities against civilians of the nation against which he is fighting.	24%	23%

Table 2

1. The most appropriate goal of the criminal justice system should be punishment.
2. If murderers were executed, the incidence of murders would decrease.
3. Some criminals cannot be rehabilitated.
4. Anyone who commits a murder must be insane.
5. Executions are cruel and inhumane.
6. The most appropriate goal of the criminal justice system should be rehabilitation.
7. A convicted murderer should have the right to choose death over life imprisonment. ,
8. Televised executions of murderers would have a strong deterrent effect for murder.
9. Executing a criminal is never justified.
10. A life sentence with no chance of parole is a more severe punishment than death.
11. The punishment should fit the crime, not the criminal.
12. The punishment should fit the criminal, not the crime.
13. Executions would be applied more often to the poor and underprivileged than to the middle classes.
14. The mentally incompetent should not be executed.
15. The death penalty statutes should be made similar in every state in the USA.

REFERENCES

Feild, H. Attitudes toward rape. *J. Pers. Soc. Psychol.*, 1978, 36, 156-179.

Lester, D. Why do people become police officers. *J. Police Sci. Admin.*, 1983, 11, 170-174.

Appendix 2

ATTITUDES TOWARD RAPE AND CAPITAL PUNISHMENT

DAVID LESTER

IN ORDER TO explore whether attitudes toward capital punishment were related to attitudes toward rape, a questionnaire was completed anonymously by 70 students in social science courses. There were 38 males and 32 females, with a mean age of 23.6 years (SD = 5.4). Students were given the Feild (1978) pro-rape scale, a list of nine crimes for which the respondent could indicate "yes" or "no" for execution as a fitting punishment, and an eight-item scale of attitudes toward capital punishment in a Likert-type format.

Scores favoring capital punishment on the Likert scale were significantly correlated with the number of crimes for which execution was checked as a desirable punishment (Pearson r = 0.62, p < 0.001). However, attitudes toward capital punishment and the number of crimes for which execution was checked as a desirable punishment were not related to having a pro-rape attitude (r's = 0.01 and 0.02 respectively). (Incidentally, age was not related to attitudes toward capital punishment or rape, but males checked more crimes as deserving of execution and had a stronger pro-rape attitude.)

Thus, these results indicate that attitudes toward capital punishment were not related to attitudes toward rape.

REFERENCE

Feild, H. Attitudes toward rape. *J. Pers. Soc. Psychol.*, 36: 156-179, 1978.

The capital punishment items were:
1. If murderers were executed the incidence of murders would decrease.
2. Executions are cruel and inhumane.
3. A convicted murderer should have the right to choose death over life imprisonment.
4. Televised executions of murderers would have a strong deterrent effect for murder.
5. Executing a criminal is never justified.
6. A life sentence with no chance of parole is a more severe punishment than death.
7. Executions would be applied more often to the poor and underprivileged than to the middle classes.
8. The mentally incompetent should not be executed.

The crimes were:
Murder
Rape
Kidnapping
Political assassination
Espionage
Child abuse resulting in death
Mass murder
A person who has murdered more than once
Murder of a child

THE DETERRENT EFFECT OF EXECUTIONS ON MURDER: ANALYSES BY STATE EACH YEAR FROM 1930 TO 1965 IN THE CONTINENTAL USA*

DAVID LESTER

THE PRESENT analyses of the deterrent effect of executions on murder were designed to explore the effects of executions in a given state in a given year on the increase or decrease in the number of homicides in that state in the following year.

The analyses utilize the following data:

(a) The number of executions in each state each year,

(b) The number of deaths due to homicide and non-negligent manslaughter in each state each year,

(c) For each continental state of the USA, and

(d) For the time period 1930 to 1965.

Study One:
The Effect of One or More Executions Versus no Executions

Data on the number of homicidal deaths by year and state were obtained from *Mortality Statistics* for 1930-1936, and from *Vital Statistics of the United States* for 1937 onwards. Data on executions by year and state were obtained from the *National Prisoner Statistics.*

Each state each year was classified as an execution state or as a non-execution state based upon whether one or more persons were executed in that state during that year. Then, the number of homicides in that state during that year and the following year were noted,

---

*Presented at a Georgia State University Conference On Capital Punishment, 1980.

and the change classified as an increase, a decrease, or a tie. These constitute the basic data.

The technique answers the question "Does an execution in a given state in a given year lower the number of homicides committed in that state during the following year?"

Results

The data are first presented by state (see Table 1). It can be seen that, overall, if a state executed one or more persons in a given year, then there was a drop in the number of homicides 54.0% of the time in the following year. If no one was executed, the number dropped in only 44.0 %. The deterrent effect was found in 28 states, not found in 12, and could not be examined in nine, since they either never executed anyone or else they executed at least one person each year. This difference is statistically significant (one-tailed binomial $p = 0.009$). The only state for which the deterrent effect was statistically significant was Arkansas (Fisher exact $p = 0.024$).

This difference was noted for years in which the incidence of homicide was rising (45.7% versus 40.3%) and for years in which the incidence of homicide was decreasing (58.8% versus 53.7%).

By year, the deterrent effect of executions was also noted (see Table 2), with the drop in homicides occurring after 53.5% of the occasions in which a state executed at least one person and only 46.7% of the occasions in which no one was executed. The deterrent effect of executions was found in 21 of the years but not in 14 (binomial $p = 0.16$). The deterrent effect was statistically significant in 1954 and 1962, but statistically significant in the opposite direction in 1945.

Table 1

THE EFFECT OF AN EXECUTION IN ONE YEAR ON THE NUMBER OF
HOMICIDES IN THE FOLLOWING YEAR, BY STATE, FOR 1930-1965.

State	After an Execution Year		After a Non-Execution Year			Predicted Direction
	Decrease	Increase	Decrease	Increase	Ties	
ME	–	–	–	–	–	–
NH	1	0	15	14	5	yes
VT	2	1	15	9	8	yes
MA	5	7	9	14	0	yes
RI	–	–	–	–	–	–
CT	5	7	9	12	2	no
NY	19	11	1	2	2	yes
NJ	13	10	5	7	0	yes
PA	17	12	2	4	0	yes
OH	23	10	0	2	0	yes
IN	9	9	7	10	0	yes
IL	14	9	5	7	0	yes
MI	–	–	–	–	–	–
WI	–	–	–	–	–	–
MN	–	–	–	–	–	–
IA	7	4	12	12	0	yes
MO	15	10	5	4	1	yes
ND	–	–	–	–	–	–
SD	0	1	13	17	4	no
NE	2	2	12	17	2	yes
KS	5	2	15	12	1	yes
DE	4	3	12	13	3	yes
MD	11	14	4	5	1	no
DC	8	10	8	8	1	no
VA	15	14	3	3	0	yes
WV	12	7	7	7	2	yes
NC	11	18	3	3	0	no
SC	16	13	1	4	1	yes
GA	–	–	–	–	–	–
FL	17	18	0	0	0	no
KY	16	10	3	6	0	yes
TN	12	10	6	7	0	yes
AL	16	16	1	1	0	–
MS	18	14	2	1	0	no
AR	18	10	1	6	0	yes
LA	13	16	4	2	0	no
OK	13	9	5	7	1	yes
TX	–	–	–	–	–	–
MT	2	3	15	15	0	no
ID	2	0	14	16	3	yes
WY	4	1	12	13	5	yes
CO	11	10	8	5	1	no
NM	3	3	14	13	2	no
AZ	10	9	6	10	0	yes
UT	7	4	12	11	1	yes
NV	6	13	6	7	3	no
WA	12	10	4	7	2	yes
OR	6	5	10	12	2	yes
CA	15	19	0	1	0	yes
TOTALS	415	354	286	326	53	

Table 2

THE EFFECT OF AN EXECUTION IN ONE YEAR ON THE NUMBER OF
HOMICIDES IN THE FOLLOWING YEAR, FOR ALL STATES, BY YEAR

State	After an Execution Year		After a Non-Execution Year		Ties	Predicted Direction
	Decrease	*Increase*	*Decrease*	*Increase*		
1930	9	21	9	9	0	no
1931	16	12	10	7	3	no
1932	10	17	10	9	2	no
1933	16	14	12	7	0	no
1934	24	3	17	5	0	yes
1935	18	10	13	7	1	no
1936	20	10	10	8	1	yes
1937	22	6	12	5	3	yes
1938	18	12	11	8	0	yes
1939	16	13	12	7	1	no
1940	20	9	12	8	0	yes
1941	15	11	7	10	6	yes
1942	23	6	11	8	1	yes
1943	16	12	8	10	3	yes
1944	6	20	5	17	1	yes
1945	3	27	7	10	2	no
1946	19	11	8	7	4	yes
1947	15	14	6	11	3	yes
1948	12	9	11	10	7	yes
1949	14	11	13	9	2	no
1950	17	6	14	9	3	yes
1951	4	22	7	15	1	no
1952	17	7	12	12	1	yes
1953	9	11	13	15	1	no
1954	16	3	10	18	2	yes
1955	9	10	18	11	1	no
1956	12	8	9	19	1	yes
1957	8	12	18	9	2	no
1958	6	9	10	24	0	yes
1959	5	10	12	20	2	no
1960	11	9	11	14	4	yes
1961	3	14	12	17	3	no
1962	10	7	7	24	1	yes
1963	4	7	11	24	3	yes
1964	3	5	12	29	0	yes
Total	446	388	380	432		
	53.5%		46.8%			

(The difference between the total data by state and by year are due
to the inclusion in the latter analysis of the eight states for which a state
analysis could not be performed.)

Discussion

Examination of the results shows that there is evidence for a weak effect from executions in lowering the homicide rate. If a state executed one or more persons in a given year, there was a greater probability that the homicide rate would drop the following year than if the state did not execute anyone. Since most states were executing only a very small proportion of murderers, it is to be expected that the deterrent effect would be small. If, for example, all those convicted of first-degree homicide were executed, the deterrent effect might be larger.

Study Two: The Deterrent Effect of Executions as a Function of the Number of Executions

The previous analysis indicated that one or more executions in a state in a given year were more likely to lead to a drop in the number of homicides in the following year than were zero executions. The present analysis reports on whether the **number** of executions in a state in a given year was related to this deterrent effect.

Method

The data were obtained from the same sources as in Study One. For each state each year the number of executions was noted and whether the number of homicides decreased or increased in that state in the following year.

Results

The number of increases and decreases for different numbers of executions in a given year in the states is shown in Table 3. It can be seen that for 1–8 executions in a given year, the number of homicides in the following year decreased on 367 of the 709 occasions or 51.8%. For 9–16 executions in a given year, the number of homicides in the following year decreased on 74 of the 107 occasions or 69.2%. For 17–23 executions in a given year, the number of homicides in the following year decreased on 11 of the 18 occasions or 61.1%.

Table 3
THE NUMBER OF INCREASES AND DECREASES IN HOMICIDES
FROM YEAR n TO YEAR n + 1 AS A FUNCTION OF THE NUMBER
OF EXECUTIONS IN YEAR n.

Number of Executions	Increases	Decreases	Ties	% of Decreases
1	111	110	6	50
2	79	74	3	52
3	42	35	2	55
4	42	45	1	48
5	32	30		52
6	18	24	1	43
7	21	11	1	66
8	22	13		63
9	18	9		67
10	16	7		70
11	13	3		81
12	8	2		80
13	6	5		55
14	5	3		62
15	4	3		57
16	4	1		80
17	2	2		50
18	4	0		100
19	0	2		0
20	2	2		50
21	1	0		100
22	1	0		100
23	1	1		50

Discussion

It can be seen that the more executions in a state in a given year the greater the likelihood of a drop in the number of homicides the following year, up to a point. The data for 17–23 executions are discrepant. These data are based on a small number of cases and so the estimate of the percentage is less reliable than for the other instances. Furthermore, these data come from a select few states which executed large numbers of criminals (Alabama, California, Georgia, New York, North Carolina, and Texas).

Study Three: The Deterrent Effect of Executions as a Function of the Proportion of Executions

The present analyses examine the relationship between the, **proportion** of executions to homicides in a state in a given year and increases and decreases in the number of homicides in the following year.

Method

The data were obtained from the same sources as the previous analyses. For each state each year, the number of executions was expressed as a proportion of the number of homicides in that state that year. For each proportion, the number of decreases and increases in the number of homicides in that state the following year was noted.

Results and Discussion

The likelihood of a decrease in the number of homicides after a year with a given proportion of executions is shown in Table 4.

It can be seen that the higher the proportion of murderers executed in a given year as compared to the number of homicides that year, the more likely a drop in the number of homicides in the following year, except for the highest proportions of all. The reasons for this reversal at the highest proportions are not clear. All of the states contributing to this category were ones with small numbers of homicides each year (Arizona, Connecticut, Delaware, Iowa, Idaho, Nevada, South Dakota, Utah, Vermont, Washington and Wyoming).

Table 4

THE LIKELIHOOD OF A DECREASE IN THE NUMBER OF HOMICIDES IN A STATE FROM YEAR n TO YEAR n + 1 AS A FUNCTION OF THE PROPORTION OF EXECUTIONS IN YEAR n.

Proportion of Executions to Homicides in Year n	*Likelihood of a Decrease in the Number of Homicides in Year n + 1*		
	Decreases	*Increases*	*Percentage of Decreases*
0.001 - 0.009	119	111	51.7
0.010 - 0.019	233	114	53.8
0.020 - 0.029	82	72	53.2
0.030 - 0.039	43	27	61.4
0.040 - 0.049	25	11	69.4
0.050+	34	44	43.6

Study Four: The Deterrent Effect of Executions on the Number of Homicides Committed in the Same Year

In Study One, the deterrent effect of one or more executions in a state in a given year upon the number of homicides in the state was examined. In this study, the deterrent effect of one or more executions in a state in a given year upon the number of homicides in the same year (as compared to the number in the next year) was examined. This was done because, if the deterrent effect of an execution upon the homicide rate is short-term, then it would be expected to be found in the year in which the execution takes place or shortly thereafter. Study One did not examine the immediate deterrent effect, and so Study Four was conducted to remedy this omission.

Method

The sources of data were the same as in Study One. Each state was examined each year, and each instance was classified as to whether or not an execution took place. Then the number of homicides in the state in the year that the execution took place was compared to the number in the prior year. (Study One examined the number in each year that an execution took place as compared to the number in the following year.)

Results

For years in which no execution took place, the number of homicides was less than the number in the previous year for 400 of the 840 instances (47.6%). For years in which one or more executions took place, the number of homicides was less than the number in the previous year for 427 of the 808 instances (52.8%)(see Table 5).

Thus, the deterrent effect of an execution is found in the year in which the execution takes place.

Table 5
THE EFFECT OF AN EXECUTION IN ONE YEAR ON THE NUMBER OF
HOMICIDES IN THE SAME YEAR, BY STATE, FOR 1930-1965.

State	During an Execution Year		During a Non-Execution Year			Predicted Direction
	Decrease	Increase	Decrease	Increase	Ties	
ME	–	–	16	16	3	–
NH	0	1	16	13	5	no
VT	0	1	17	9	8	no
MA	7	5	7	16	0	yes
RI	–	–	15	18	2	–
CT	4	8	10	11	2	no
NY	19	10	1	3	2	yes
NJ	13	9	5	8	0	yes
PA	16	12	3	4	0	yes
OH	22	10	1	2	0	yes
IN	7	10	9	9	0	no
IL	14	8	5	8	0	yes
MI	–	–	16	19	0	–
WI	–	–	16	18	1	–
MN	–	–	16	18	1	–
IA	8	3	11	13	0	yes
MO	15	9	4	6	1	yes
ND	–	–	16	16	3	–
SD	–	–	13	18	4	–
NE	1	3	13	16	2	no
KS	2	6	18	8	1	no
DE	4	3	12	13	3	yes
MD	13	12	2	7	1	yes
VA	15	13	3	4	0	yes
WV	10	8	9	6	2	no
NC	13	15	1	6	0	yes
SC	14	14	3	3	1	–
GA	14	19	0	1	1	yes
KY	16	9	3	7	0	yes
TN	13	8	5	9	0	yes
AL	15	17	2	1	0	no
MS	19	22	1	3	0	yes
AR	15	12	4	4	0	yes
LA	15	13	2	5	0	yes
OK	11	11	7	5	1	no
TX	17	14	1	0	0	no
MT	4	1	13	17	0	yes
ID	0	2	16	14	3	no
WY	2	1	14	13	5	yes
CO	14	7	5	8	1	yes
NM	2	4	15	12	2	no
UT	4	7	15	8	1	no
NV	9	10	3	10	3	yes
WA	12	9	4	8	2	yes
OR	3	8	13	9	2	no
CA	15	18	0	2	0	yes
FL	17	17	0	1	0	yes
AZ	6	12	10	7	0	no
DC	7	10	9	8	1	no
Totals	427	381	400	440	64	

Study Five: Number of Years With Executions and Number of Years With Decrease in the Number of Homicides, by State for 1930-1965

The first three studies have indicated that if a state executes one or more persons in a given year, then the state will be more likely to experience a decrease in the number of homicides in the following year. This analysis sought to see whether states which had more years with one or more executions also had more decreases in the number of homicides from year n to year n + 1 for the period 1930-1965.

Method

Each of 48 continental states was included in this analysis, except for Texas for which data were not available for the complete period from 1930 to 1965. For this 35 year period, for each state, the number of years with one or more executions and the number of decreases in the number of homicides from year n to year n + 1 (with n going from 1930 to 1964) were noted. These two numbers were correlated over the 47 states included in the analysis.

Results and Discussion

The product-moment correlation between the number of years with executions and the number of year-to-year decreases in the number of homicides was 0.30 (one tailed $p < 0.025$). Thus, states with more years in which one or more executions took place experienced more year-to-year decreases in the number of homicides.

Conclusions

The analyses in this paper have departed from other recent analyses in several major respects. First, and foremost, the analyses have utilized simple statistical techniques. Recent papers by other investigators have utilized instead complex statistical techniques of analysis with several consequences. Other researchers often criticize the statistical analyses used and the statistical assumptions made by each other. The more the analysis of the problem becomes embroiled in arcane statistical techniques, the less amenable are the results to all interested parties. Furthermore, the suspicion is that a resort to complex statistical techniques is a result of the fact that the deterrent effect of executions is minute, too minute to show up in simple analyses of the data. The aim in this report has been to demonstrate the deterrent effect of executions in a manner that any intelligent person can comprehend.

This report also differs from some other studies in that it focuses upon the states of the USA. It seems inappropriate to study the nation as a whole, for there is no reason to expect that an execution in California will have any impact on a murderer in Maine. Furthermore, the report follows a recent trend in focussing on executions rather than the existence of a death penalty. A death penalty would have little deterrent effect it is never used, and so executions are the more appropriate focus for study.

The present study used the absolute number of homicides each year in each state as reported by the Center for Vital Statistics. The data on murder reported by the FBI have been criticized for their inaccuracies, and data from the mortality statistics of the USA provided by the Center for Vital Statistics are considered more accurate. Absolute numbers of deaths from homicide were used simply for ease in these preliminary analyses. Currently rates of murder for each state each year are being computed and will be used in future analyses. However, in the vast majority of cases, increases (or decreases) in the absolute number of homicides in a state from year to year are paralleled by similar increases (or decreases) in the computed rate of homicide. The use of rates will have minimal effects on the results here. (For example, in 1930 in New York state there were 712 deaths from homicide and in 1931 there were 821. The corresponding rates are 5.63 and 6.39, both types of statistics indicating an increase.

The results of the five analyses presented here indicate that executions do have a deterrent effect on homicide. The effect is quite small and the effect appears to break down for large numbers of executions. The reason for this latter finding is not clear. It may be a result of the small number of cases involving large numbers of executions, causing these data points to be less reliably estimated. It may be that the few states involved are not representative of the nation as a whole. Or it may be that the weak deterrent effect of executions does break down when executions become more common. Further research may differentiate between these alternatives.

Statistical Note

It could be argued that since the data constitutes the universe and not a sample, then no statistical tests of significance are appropriate.

The 1646 data points (35 years by 58 states and Washington, DC, with missing data for Texas) are not equivalent and independent events. Thus, tests such as an overall chi-square are not appropriate.

If we leave aside the first objection, then the only test of significance that seems appropriate is a t-test for related samples applied to the data in Table 1, Table 2 and Table 5 separately. The percentage of decreases for each state (in Tables 1 and 5) and for each year (in Table 2) after execution years and after non-execution years separately were calculated and the t-test applied to these data.

The results of these tests were:

	mean percentage of decreases				
	after execution year	after non-execution year	t	df	two-tailed p
Table 1	55.6%	43.5%	3.49	39	< 0.01
Table 2	52.1%	48.6%	1.21	34	ns
Table 3	48.4%	42.6%	1.21	41	ns

Appendix 4

THE DETERRENT EFFECT OF EXECUTIONS ON THE HOMICIDE RATE IN THE USA

DAVID LESTER

IN THE INVESTIGATION of the deterrent effect of executions on the homicide rate in the USA, one approach that has received a great deal of attention has involved the study of the executions in the USA as a whole since the 1930s and the relationship between various measures of this punishment upon the total homicide rate. The procedure used by Ehrlich (1975) and several critics of his work involves including a selection of social indicators into a multiple regression analysis and determining whether an index of the executions carried out each year adds a significant component to the equation predicting the homicide rate over time (a temporal correlation). The problem with this procedure is that the USA is not a homogeneous nation. Each state has its own laws, judicial process and patterns of administration and implementation of these laws and processes. A study of the USA as a whole misses this complexity. For the sake of providing a concrete example, would an execution of a murderer in California be expected to have any impact on the homicide rate in Michigan where capital punishment has been abolished?

An alternative approach has been to carry out cross-sectional correlations. A given year is taken, say 1960. The homicide rates of each state in 1960 are the target variable. Various social indicators are included in a multiple regression analysis, including indices of the execution practices in the various states. Then it is determined whether the index of executions adds a significant component to the equation predicting the state homicide rates. This approach has been utilized by Forst (1977).

This latter approach makes good sense. However, it seems unnecessary to restrict the analysis to one year. Data are available for each state for the period from 1930 on. Lester (1980) carried out a crude analysis to show that during the period from 1930 to 1965, if a state executed one or more criminals in a given year, then there was a 54.2 percent chance that the number of homicides in that state would decrease the following year; if the state executed no one in a given year then there was only a 46.7 percent chance that the number of homicides in that state would decrease in the following year. However, the level of analysis conducted by Lester could be improved by calculating the correlation coefficients accurately between measures of each state's execution practices in one year and the changes in the homicide rate from year to year. The present paper sought to illustrate this technique and to examine the results obtained for their implications for the deterrent effect of executions on homicidal behavior.

Method

Data on executions and homicides for each continental state were obtained for the period 1930-1965, with the exception of Texas for which data were missing for the years 1930-1932. Years prior to 1930 were not included because of the reduced number of states reporting the required information. Years after 1965 were not included because of the rarity of executions in the USA after 1965.

Three measures of execution practices were used: (E1) the percentage of executions in a state in a given year as a proportion of the number of homicides in the state in that year, (E2) the presence of one or more executions in a state in a given year versus no executions (expressed as a binary variable coded as 1 and 0) and (E3) the actual number of executions in each state each year.

Two measures of the homicide rate change were used: (H1) whether the homicide rate increased or decreased from one year to the next in each state (expressed as a binary variable coded as 1 or 0); and (H2) the actual change in the homicide rate from one year to the next in each state.

The measures of execution practices were correlated with the measures of homicide rate changes using product-moment correlation coefficients. Three time lags were used: zero, one and two years. For example, the measure of homicide rate change for 1930-1931 was correlated first with the measure of execution practices in 1930 over all 48 continental states, then with the measure of execution practices in

1931, and finally with the measure of execution practices in 1932. For this last time lag, no deterrent effect could possibly be expected. Executions in 1932 should not affect homicidal behavior in 1930 and 1931. Thus, this time lag was included as a check on the meaningfulness of the patterns of correlations obtained.

These correlations were calculated for each possible homicide rate change in the period studied, beginning with 1930-1931 and ending with 1964-1965. For each combination of execution practice measure and homicide rate change measure, the 35 correlation coefficients were averaged. (For the two year lag correlations, only 34 correlation coefficients were calculated for each combination.)

Results

The average correlation coefficients for each combination of execution/homicide rate change indices and for each time lag period are shown in Table 1. It can be seen that very slight, but statistically significant deterrent effects from executions were found for four of the six tests using a zero-year time lag, five of the six tests using a one-year time lag, and only two of the six tests using a two-year time lag. (Deterrent effects would be expected for only the time lags of zero or one year and not for a time lag of two years.)

Thus, the results seem to provide support for a very slight deterrent effect of executions on homicide rates.

Table 1

THE AVERAGE CORRELATIONS BETWEEN INDICES OF EXECUTIONS
AND INDICES OF CHANGES IN THE HOMICIDE RATES
FOR ALL 48 CONTINENTAL STATES

	Zero time lag (e. g., executions in 1930/homicide rate change 1930-1931)	*One year time lag* (e. g., executions in 1931/homicide rate change 1930-1931)	*Two year time lag* (e. g., executions in 1932/homicide rate change 1930-1931)
E1/H1	−0.016	−0.046*	−0.001
E1/H2	+0.027	−0.081***	+0.039
E2/H1	−0.069***	−0.048*	−0.041
E2/H2	−0.060**	−0.044*	−0.019
E3/H1	−0.078***	−0.056*	−0.044*
E3/H2	−0.075***	−0.039	−0.046*

* one-tailed p < 0.05   ** one-tailed p < 0.01   *** one-tailed p < 0.005

Discussion

The data presented in this paper are consistent with a deterrent effect from executions on the homicide rate. States with more executions in a given year were more likely to experience a drop in the homicide rate in the following year than states with fewer executions for the period 1930 to 1965. The association was, however, extremely small, though statistically significant. In addition, it was shown that the association was consistent with a deterrent effect by demonstrating that executions in a given year were not related to changes in the homicide rate in the years prior to the given year.

Although the associations between executions and changes in the homicide rate were small, it must be remembered that only a very small proportion of murderers were executed. For example, North Carolina executed 23 murders in 1936, when there were 392 homicides, a ratio of 0.059. In other years, the ratio for North Carolina was much smaller. If the probability that a murderer would be executed were higher, then the deterrent effect of executions might be greater.

REFERENCES

Ehrlich, I. The deterrent effect of capital punishment. *Amer. Econ. Rev.*, 65: 397-417, 1975.

Forst, B. E. The deterrent effect of capital punishment: a cross-state analysis of the 1960's. *Minn. Law Review*, 61: 743-767, 1977.

Lester, D. The deterrent effect of executions on murder: analyses by state each year from 1930 to 1965 in the continental USA. Conference on Capital Punishment, Georgia State University, 1980.

AUTHOR INDEX

SUBJECT INDEX